5 FEARLESS DAYS

5

FEARLESS DAYS

WRITE THAT BOOK, CODE THAT APP, LEARN THAT SKILL

IN 120 HOURS

MICHAEL KNUDSEN

L8 BLOOMER PRESS

5 FEARLESS DAYS

Cover design and formatting: L8 Bloomer Press

First Edition 2026

Free gifts for readers at:
www.5fearlessdays.com

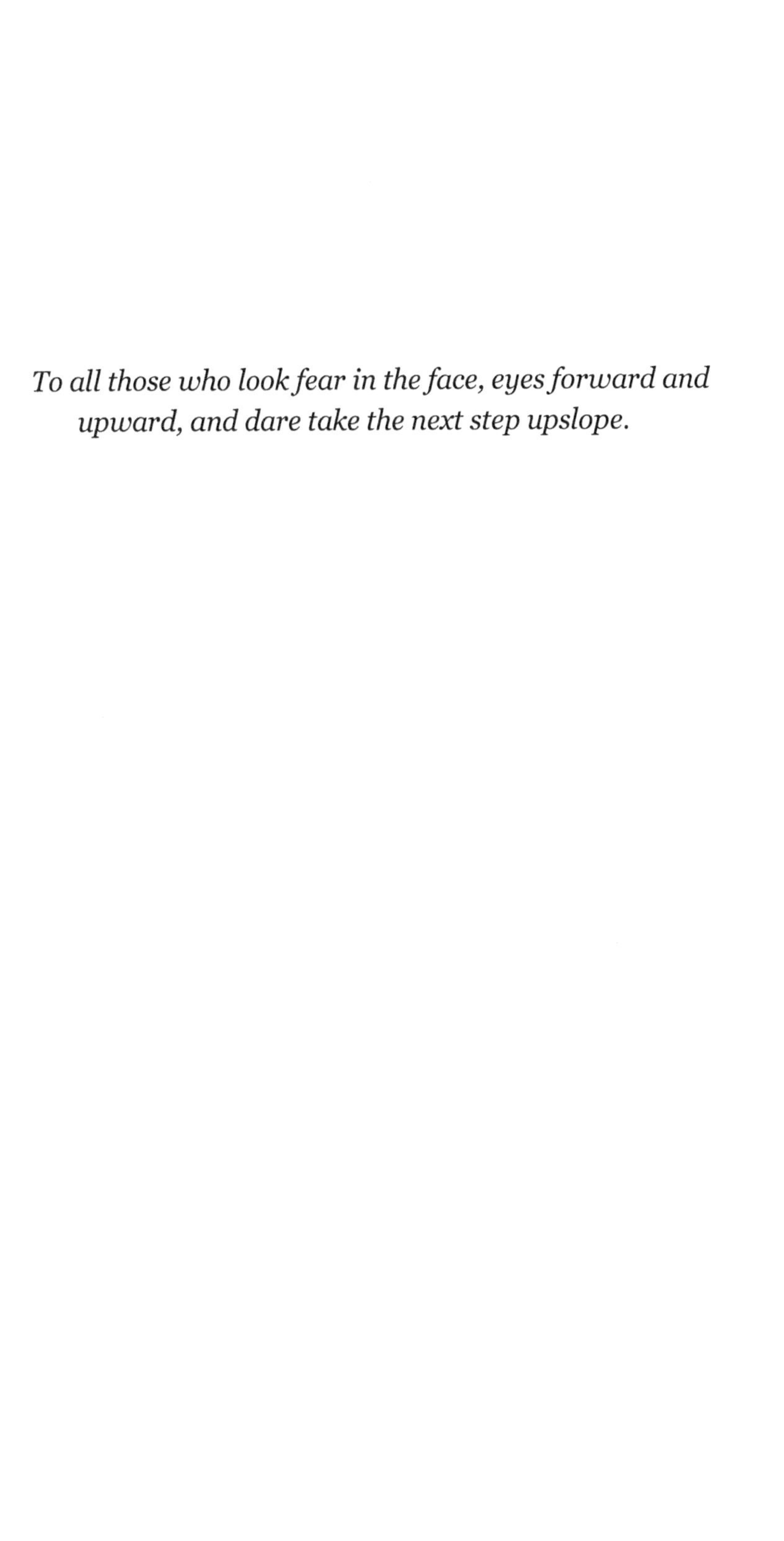

To all those who look fear in the face, eyes forward and upward, and dare take the next step upslope.

Contents

Preface

This isn't a book about making money.

You'll find no specifics here about "$10k a month within a year" or "100 leads per day".

The people who write about those things have their own genre, and they make a huge assumption: You already have something worth the money they're saying you'll make if you follow their guidance, or having a big online following can be converted into your prosperity and endless happiness.

They assume the "stuff" you'll offer in exchange for money from your customers' bank accounts is already there, with a big "for sale" sign on it, ready to go.

The service. The book. The software. The art.

But what if it's still stuck in your imagination? What if you have a great idea but haven't actually created the product yet?

What's the point of reading books about sales, marketing, big money and morning routines when you have yet to create something of value?

This book is about **making the stuff**. It's meant to be read *and acted on **before*** you read the books on how to distribute and profit from your stuff. **_You can't ship what you don't have._**

This book makes a simple and bold assertion: One decision followed by five days of carefully planned, dedicated effort is enough to accomplish something significant to you and to transform your life in lasting ways.

The purchase price of this book will wind up being either the highest-leverage investment you make this year, or a complete waste of money.

There is no middle ground.

As the author of a "motivational" book, my reputation is on the line. If you don't do anything as a result of reading it, the sunk costs include my time and your money. The price of this book is roughly the same as a movie ticket. If all you get from it is entertainment, you may as well trudge off to the multiplex, popcorn bucket in hand.

Yet I have a sky-high degree of confidence if you actually do what this book outlines, you will look back on this purchase as a pivot point. You might even thank me.

But if you never embark on a challenge culminating in this prescribed five-day journey, or you start one and quit on it, it's likely two things combine to result in a stillborn transformation:

1. You haven't really made a decision, which is a choice paired with commitment. Maybe it's a pattern in your life, and it hasn't yet been interrupted.
2. My words weren't strong enough to persuade you to interrupt the pattern.

I'll do *my* part in these pages.

Gifted or cursed from early childhood with "a way with words" (eyes often roll with the delivery of this compliment), I will pull out all stops and hold nothing back.

Well, I'll hold back the profanity. Most of it. A rare and tactical "damn" or "hell" can really amp a sentence. But the stronger stuff, the whiskey and vodka of the cussing world? You can leave this one out where the kids will find it.

In fact, the sooner in life anyone reads and implements the contents of this book, the less regret they may experience in life.

Wow.

Did I really just imply *"if you don't do what my book says, you're gonna regret it?"*

This isn't about ego.

I'm just someone possessed of an unshakable belief: I believe human creativity is the last best hope for a dying civilization and planet. Not government. Not philosophy. Not charismatic leaders. Not AI. Just good old-fashioned imagination followed closely by execution. I'm no atheist-humanist. I believe in God. His work will be done. But we all have a stewardship in this world. We're agents. Within limits, it's in our hands. It's our given dominion. We can get ourselves out of so many of the messes we've gotten ourselves into by **making new things that weren't there before**. Things that move people. Things that improve lives. This thread runs through history if you look for it.

I make daring assumptions about anyone picking up this book. You want better from yourself. You know you're capable of it. You've got great things to do, and you'll do them.

Someday.

But more than procrastination stops you.

You feel like a recipe missing a vital ingredient or two. You perceive those ingredients as "out there", and believe if you can only find them and stir them in, deliciousness is inevitable.

So you read, watch and listen to the best. You really do listen. You've taken in a lot. You may even feel like you could write your own motivational book - or at least something big, bold and ambitious.

But you haven't.

Whatever it is, it's still in there, rattling around, battling "demons".

One of those demons is Time. He's an elusive beast who always seems to lurk around the next corner. You'll capture this beast and compel him to serve you. The alternative is to find yourself one day shaking your frosted head and whimpering about how he got away from you.

We'll also confront the monsters Fear, Doubt and Distraction, all servants of the Final Boss, *Resistance*, within these pages. These are lifelong shadows haunting you even after you think you've long exorcised them.

We'll address these gargoyles for what they are. We'll externalize them. Sure, they originate and gain strength from within you, but getting them out in the open is the only way to take clear shots at them.

We can't dwell on them for long. They only deserve as much attention as it takes to protect you from them for five fleeting rotations of the earth on its axis.

Five short days.

It's a tiny investment of time for anyone, with the possible exceptions of the terminally ill and chronically aged.

Five days is 17% of a month, 1.4% of a year, and 0.14% of a decade.

Global statistics show the average adult will spend five days' worth of waking hours streaming and scrolling social media *every two weeks.*

Be honest: With a gun to your head, you'd come up with five days. Your addiction to the dopamine shots from the pixel circus on your phone would be cured and time would multiply like the bread and fish coming out of a basket in a Galilee field.

There is no gun to your head.

Along with being a mixer of metaphors to shame a Japanese bartender, I'm a pacifist. I step with vigilant care down sidewalks where ants are present.

But there is this book.

Its purpose is to be weaponized.

The demons in your path should be quaking in their boots about now.

Demons wear boots?

Here we go. I almost clicked off my draft to ask some AI to make me an image of a demon in boots. It would have taken ten seconds, and we might have shared a laugh. A nice little bonding moment.

I'm not even done with the preface!

So you're not alone in what you face. Here I am, the "author" (the root of *authority*), and I'm dancing around distraction within the first couple of pages of my book about five days of intense focus.

No author is perfect.

I have my own stories about what I've done in five days, and I'll share them within. I stumbled into the power of this time frame somewhat accidentally, but once I discovered it, I used it over and over. This book was drafted during one five-day challenge and finished for publication during another!

My experience prompted a question: Is it just me, or is there something universal about this idea of a decision followed by preparation for and execution of intensity over a handful of days?

So I offered to coach people for free through five-day decision-anchored challenges, with a focus on creative projects they assumed would take months or years.

Verdict?

As long as the decision is real and there is a temporary willingness to set aside the distracting darlings of the digital domain, it works.

In the process of working with people, each of them distinct, intelligent, creative and beautiful individuals, the framework in this book emerged and has matured.

Sure, you can wing it.

Keep reading self-help, watching videos and listening to podcasts, hoping the sheer volume of wonderful ideas one day reaches critical mass and forces you to do something. Someday, somehow, something so shiny your creative juices spontaneously combust and make your dreams come true.

Yeah, probably not gonna happen.

Instead, why not narrow your focus to a period of time you perceive as almost insignificant - five days - and silence everything but the thing inside you most needing a voice? Then hone that skill over repetition so you become the master of your time - at all times, not just during scheduled challenges.

I've watched people complete things in five days they had *thought about* for years prior to the challenge. Books, memoirs, courses, breakthrough modules of code.

All nothing but figments of their imagination before. Figments haunting and persisting for years, sometimes decades.

Then, less than a freakin' week later? Tangible assets. Satisfying proofs of an individual being's gifts and purpose. Evidence of an established creative identity.

The difference?

One decision.

Five days.

Before and After

How I Wrote a Novel in Five Days

I've been a writer since I was handed a No. 2 pencil and asked to scratch out my name on pulpy kindergarten paper.

At age seven I made a set of illustrated storybooks on folded scrap paper for my mother's eyes only. She cherished them and encouraged me to make more.

At thirteen I made a comic book serial called *The Mighty Micromartians* for my friends in the neighborhood. They loved my wacky alien characters (who were really just cool teenagers in disguise) and asked for more.

At twenty-one I wrote short stories for a creative writing class in college. The professor pulled me aside and encouraged me to go deeper.

While still in school I worked part-time at an old-school formalwear shop near campus. The owner had been renting and selling tuxedos for more than forty years. My co-workers were a remarkable cast of characters, and some interpersonal drama or conflict was always underway. I kept thinking, *there's a story here. There's an* epic *story here.*

So of all people, I'd be the one to write that story, right?

It was 1988. I got married, graduated. Moved on to a job calculated to pay bigger bills. Shouldered responsibility commensurate with my salary. Came home exhausted after long shifts each night.

Writing? I dabbled once in a while, when things were caught up and I had "nothing better to do". I read an enormous number of books, as procrastinating writers tend to do. Not just self-help and literary fiction, oh no. I contributed to the fortunes of publishing empires like those of Dean Koontz, Stephen King, John Grisham and Robert Jordan.

Prosperous, speculative, and impossibly prolific writers.

I fantasized about being like them. Imagine being financially independent from writing alone!

And yet, I connected zero dots and remained in a perpetual La-La Land.

I became a Tomorrowist.

One who sees a bright future ahead, but has lost sight of his own part in creating it. Somehow, somewhere, with some fuzzy benevolent intervention, the promise of my youth would be fulfilled because, well, because it was my destiny!

Idiot.

The cheerleaders of my talent were gone.

Nobody wanted writing from me anymore, except maybe the occasional email at work to communicate with co-workers.

Other, lesser (in my mind) abilities were now in demand, and I did them well enough to be presented with periodic new rungs on a ladder headed up into cloudy, vague destinations.

Twenty years, three beautiful children, two mortgages and three promotions later, I'm sitting in a deep pool of Tomorrowism and it's become far too comfortable.

November 2009. The day before a long Thanksgiving weekend beginning on Wednesday.

I felt like a burnt husk of myself after a relentless march of ten-hour shifts as a Business Unit Manager at a large outsourcing company, running a 120-seat call center for a demanding Fortune 500 client who allows no margin for error.

The kids were out of diapers and in school, heavily involved in things like various sports and swimming lessons. My wife and I were chest-deep into the joys and sorrows of being young parents.

Busy days.

But the coming five-day weekend?

No work. No school. No sports. No lessons.

Nothing on the calendar except dinner at my mother-in-law's on Thursday afternoon and church on Sunday.

Five days.

The Tomorrowist embedded in my psyche spoke up with delight:

"Wow Mike, you really deserve this. You've been working your tail off. Now's your chance to spend some quality time with the fam, maybe even watch some football with your bros. Kick back, take some naps in the

middle of the day! There's a new Dean Koontz thriller just released. Digest a gut-busting turkey dinner in peace and comfort. This is America, dammit, and it's time to give thanks by lying around."

This sounded really good. Wholesome, you know. Family, self-care, relaxation - it was practically my patriotic duty!

But there was another voice.

One for which I'm eternally grateful. Not a loud voice. Still and small. But it wrapped its argument in an ultimatum shaking me to my core:

"Five days, Mike. You see what I see? Have you really fallen so far? have you forgotten who you are? Can you no longer recognize a gift, a blessing, a fortuitous convergence of circumstance? Are you really going to let your life go by, waiting for "retirement"? What if you get taken out by a drunk driver tomorrow or next September? Is there any accountability here?"

At this point, I prepared to stick up for myself. Actually no. I prepared to step aside and let the more rhetorically muscular *Tomorrowist* fight my battles. But the quiet voice wasn't finished:

*"Five days. You either write the freaking book, or I swear we're deleting it. Forever. It's just too much of a psychic load to carry, when we both know it's going nowhere. We can't be fully happy with this on our back. Retreat from these five days and we will **wipe** your identity as a writer - for our own good."*

This awakened things in me that had long slept. Was it true? Was I really at risk of losing what I was born with, something to which I felt I was foreordained? Could it really be taken away from me?

Then I remembered Jesus' Parable of the Bags of Gold from the Bible. How the "wicked and slothful" servant buried his money out of fear and brought it back safe and sound, with no return on investment.

Wicked. Slothful.

Was I *that guy*?

No. Not gonna happen. I snapped into motion.

I had nowhere to go. Part of the house was being remodeled and my only option was the kitchen table. I grabbed my laptop and asked my wife and kids to pretend I wasn't there. Somehow, down to the nine-year-old, they sensed what Dad needed and I got my space, right there amid the Cheerios and homework assignments. I never felt distracted or "guilted" for taking time, and I love my loved ones more for it.

Memories of those five days aren't the most vivid. All I know is I kept going. Nothing resembling "writer's block" lasted more than a minute or two because I was working in the wake of a real decision for once. I wasn't sure yet how the story would end but these characters, they just kept living their lives, day by day. Stakes and conflicts escalated, climaxed and resolved.

Sunday night after the sun went down, I clacked out the words THE END on what turned out to be over 350 double-spaced pages of draft. An average of 70 pages per day.

Miraculous? Unbelievable?

I should clarify two points:

1. This wasn't a cold start. Remember I mentioned "dabbling"? I had notebooks full of unfinished outlines, character sketches and other ideas about this novel accumulated over two decades. What I lacked was DECISION and COMMITMENT.

2. The work wasn't finished Sunday night. The manuscript would be rewritten in two more drafts and ultimately self-edited to 280 pages per the publisher's requirements. It was rejected by seven publishers before finally getting a contract more than a year later.

The second item is critical.

It's crazy obvious, but there can't be a second draft without a first, let alone a published book.

I was one dude on Wednesday. A different dude on Sunday night.

How often can you claim to be a different person after just five intervening days?

"Before Mike" scribbled a few notes here and there, daydreamed, and whimpered about the "someday" on which he'd have a finished draft.

"After Mike" not only had a finished draft, he went on to spend hundreds more hours making second and third drafts, and from there did everything else necessary to sell it to a publisher, launching social media and blogging campaigns to sell thousands of copies and get dozens of reviews on Amazon.

All of that within 10% of the span of time in which "Before Mike" did nothing but collect the notes and "ideas" of a wannabe.

This went far beyond writing. Here's a partial list of things "After Mike", forty-three years old when he was born, went on to do that "Before Mike" had no stomach for:

- Trained for and ran two marathons and a dozen shorter races.
- Earned an MBA degree at age 50.
- Climbed most of the 11,000+ foot peaks in the Wasatch mountain range.
- Taught a course at a writer's conference.
- Auditioned for, sang, danced and acted the lead role in a community musical theater production.

Dare I say I'm just getting started?

I've learned we tend to wildly underestimate what we can do in a year, let alone a decade and certainly a lifetime. And it all started with five days.

But enough about me. I'm not the hero of this book. *You* are.

Rescue Yourself from the Cult of Tomorrowism

In my story I referred to my internal "Tomorrowist" preaching of the relaxing five-day weekend ahead filled with turkey, football and naps. Then there was the alternative voice, the one I consider my "true self", speaking up to intervene. In this case, I chose wisely between my two conflicting internal counselors.

I'm reminded of those cartoons with a hapless character in the middle, a horned devil on one shoulder and a winged angel on the other, sometimes coming to blows in their desperate efforts to be the determining influence over the indecisive soul.

It's useful to give "Tomorrowism" a capital "T" and consider it a dangerous cult. One parents should protect their children from, but often don't because they themselves are so deeply brainwashed their capacity to help is undermined. It becomes family baggage, the "way things are", a generational curse traversing lifespans like alcoholism or abuse - this pattern can only be interrupted by conscious, deliberate, forceful action.

The intervention finally interrupting the Tomorrowist pattern may originate with but is never consummated by external forces.

Why? Because as an adult, ultimately, you're the only one who cares if you're wasting your life. From everyone else's perspective, you are "doing you" and following your agentic path to happiness. They're all doing the same. Who are they to interfere, to judge?

You may have respected mentors to whom you've granted powers of influence over you. Authors, teachers, podcasters, people in authority who seem to have what you want. You keep wishing, hoping what they are will somehow rub off on you, or work its way into you by osmosis and transform you. It's always on the verge of happening, but never today. Maybe with one more day of listening, reading, watching, studying - maybe *tomorrow*?

Thus we partake of the arsenic-laced Kool-Aid of Tomorrowism and look forward to a supply of seemingly inexhaustible sunrises while not even the very next one is guaranteed.

What the fervent Tomorrowist seeks is closely related to the ancient practice of alchemy, in which people tried everything from chemistry to magic spells to change base metals like lead and iron into gold. Here we are in the Twenty-First Century, and it still can't be done. As we'll discover later in Chapter Seven, your gold is not manufactured - it's a gift. You can't make, buy, borrow or steal it. But you can take what you already have and *multiply* it.

Time, however, does not grow or shrink based on anything we do, except in retrospect.

> **Nothin' lasts forever but the earth and sky**
> **It slips away**
> **And all your money won't another minute buy**
> **–Dust In the Wind, Kansas**

The unique aspect of time is that while your allotment of it cannot be elongated, it can be *improved*.

The Accessible Pivot Point: Putting Your Fingerprint on Time

My five-day writing story is just an example of someone stumbling into this idea of a pivot point. A point resolved by a decision and followed by an intense burst of creative energy and output.

A handful of days.

God created this entire planet in six days, and took the next one off. Was He tired? I doubt it. Maybe he was trying to tell us something.

What is it about "a few days" that seems so insignificant in the context of a long life, yet has the potential to be so effectual when used with precision?

For one thing, it's accessible to most people.

For my first experience with it, the only sacrifices were a few days of Thanksgiving relaxation and ignoring things like email, sports and social media.

The average employee in the U.S. accrues about 15 paid days off per year after 5 years of employment. Would you give up a third of one year's accrual to give this a spin?

"But I need those days to rest and recharge. My work is hard and I look forward to my vacations."

I understand. I really do.

I also know you have something deep within you needing to find its way out, and it's just not happening the way your life is currently structured. If you were truly determined, you'd find an hour each day you could dedicate to your "work in progress". But there are many times when most of the hour would be spent fighting distraction to reach an elusive flow state, or doing little odds and ends to fill the confetti minutes as the timer quickly runs out.

You could spend years accomplishing what could be done in five days.

If your attitude toward giving up "time off" in order to do something creative is "it's just more work I won't be paid for", you've identified the first thing you need to deal with. In your mind, you've hitched time to money.

This attitude doesn't serve a creative person.

There are three ways to get money in measured exchange for time:

1. Allow people or businesses to occupy a building you own and pay you for each month.
2. Deposit your money with a financial institution and invest it for a fixed return over time.
3. Accept salary, wages or commission from someone who will tell you exactly what to do with your time.

None of these sound remotely like writing your book, building a photography portfolio, or coding the killer app you know needs to be available to the world. However, they will allow you to eat and take warm showers while you do it.

Some of you are fortunate you're not in the position of having to win bread on a daily basis. You're supported, independent, or retired. But life tends to fill the space given it, and even without a corporate dependency, you can find yourself as "busy" as ever. You're somehow still not getting what you want done.

You Won't Manifest a Thumbtack Without Hands-on Action

Contrary to viral beliefs, you're not going to "manifest" what you want by closing your eyes and getting bossy with quantum particles.

The very word "manifest" was born in Old French through the Latin "manus" (hand) and "festus" (striking), implying "struck by the hand" or "tangible". A ship's "manifest" was a description of stuff actually in the cargo hold, pushing the hull low into the water and taking up space. You know, exotic stuff out of the East Indies rich Europeans would pay gold coin for and pirates would kill for. Stuff hauled at great cost by muscle and wind halfway around the globe.

Not stuff someone *hoped* will be there or might be there someday if enough mental work is done.

This "stuff" each of us wants to bring into reality must be seen as tangible and hand-crafted or it remains in an inaccessible, unfinished realm. It's iterated in its creation so much it seldom resembles the blueprints in the creator's imagination by the time it's made available for consumption and admiration.

The truth is, you really have no idea what you can make until you set out to make it. Until you actually send the signals from your brain causing your hands to grasp your tools and manipulate hard matter into something meaningful, and do this over enough time *meaningful material manifests.*

But the moment you set your hands to the tools, and often even before, certain fights break out in your mind. Certain dialogues. Internal conversations on repeat since some kid looked at your first grade art project and proclaimed, "that's dumb".

We'll confront the beasts of Resistance and distraction in Chapter Five.

For now, it's important to internalize why five days is a sweet spot.

You're not going to produce a *magnum opus* of literature or a product compelling the masses to hurl money at you with both hands in five days.

Those are good goals, but they're the goals of years and decades deserving a vibrant life in your subconscious mind. Sure, glance at them once day. Smile and wave. Tell them gently you're coming for them, but for now you have to go. Duty calls.

Then set them aside and pick up the shovel to break hard ground on the foundation of the palace where you'll one day let them live their best life.

Five days?

It's short enough that with proper preparation and an understanding of what we'll cover in the following chapters, success surpasses "extremely likely" and heads into "inevitable" territory.

It's short enough that the chances you'll talk yourself into feelings of wasting your time and quitting are greatly diminished.

On the other hand, it's *long enough* to get something meaningful done.

Long enough to create an undeniable, tangible, manifested *artifact* of your creative identity.

It can and should be just the beginning.

It may also unlock doors in yourself you didn't know were available to you.

This book you're holding in your hands? It's just one more artifact of my own personal creativity that frankly would not exist had I not made one very specific decision coupled with a precise, written commitment in late 2025.

So here you are, simmering in your BEFORE state. But you can almost taste what's coming AFTER.

What's the best way to start building a five-day bridge so it holds the weight of all the baggage preventing you from already being where you want to be?

Turn the page. The next chapter holds the key.

The Uphill Path Less-Traveled

The Uphill Self

Impatient to jump right into the mechanics of executing a *Five Fearless Days* challenge?

Hold your horses.

I've learned the hard way a successful five-day challenge is the result not only of careful preparation (not procrastination), but also of understanding some core principles as prerequisites.

As I explained after telling my story of drafting a novel in five days, it was more than a snap decision leading to the watershed work sprint. There were many times in the years leading up to this breakthrough where I wrote, pondered, and planned my intentions, often for an hour or more at a time. I had graduated college and learned to focus on work well enough to take on responsibilities including leadership and management of teams of more than a hundred people.

My identity as a creative writer, though hanging by a thread by November 2009, had been well-established since my childhood. My talent was latent but evident. By this time, the sense I had for my capability was murky, but it was there. My "writer identity" had not yet blossomed into "novelist" or "author" because those labels require tangible artifacts of accomplishment.

These tangible proofs, and those coveted identities, remained *uphill* from me.

Most of us are world-wise enough to know the image below bears no resemblance to reality. The indecisive, questioning creative is separated from his happy, energetic, and accomplished self by more than just time (kindly ignore the fact our "accomplished self" has repeatedly skipped leg day).

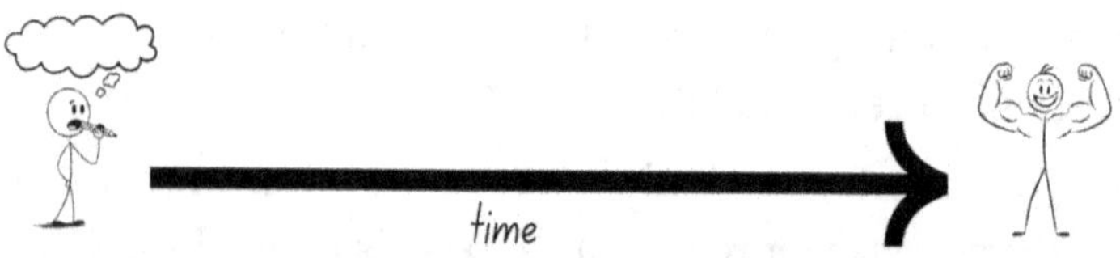

Young people, myself included for a large swath of my life, will often act like this is true, not yet knowing any better. "I'm too young", or "I don't have any experience"

are statements putting trust in the clock and calendar as the most important tools in forward progress. At this early stage of development, a person sees what their role models and mentors have and they want the same. What's not yet visible to them is *what it takes.*

The first thing we learn from our successful role models, often from their own mouths, is *"it wasn't easy, and it won't be easy for you either."*

At this point we become aware who we desire to be is about more than the passage of time. It involves defying gravity and moving to a higher plane. We begin to understand as minutes, hours and days pass, we move forward. Also, but if we're going to grow, each foot we move forward must come down on higher ground than the trailing foot below, *on average.*

This results in compounding *identity delta* over the axis of time.

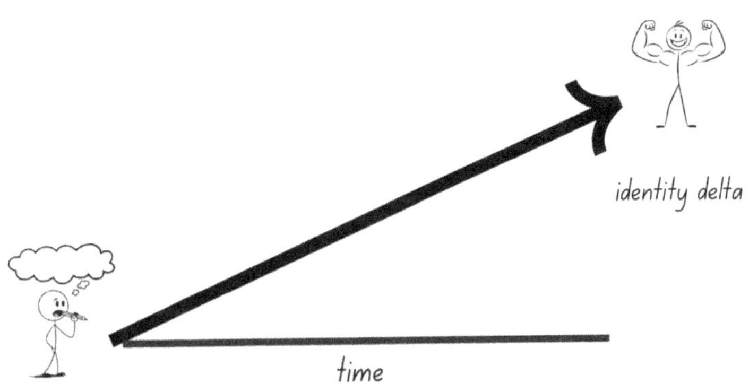

With each and every step, our eyes remain fixed on the confident smile and muscular physique of our Uphill Self standing at the summit, right?

If only it were so easy.

Instead, the uphill path is strewn with various obstacles. Some are just annoying. Steep, slippery and uneven surfaces to navigate. Others have teeth and claws, facing you with outright hostility. Yet others appear at a distance as utterly impassible, high walls with no handholds or crevices to leverage. Instead of climbing steadily, worrying only about conserving energy and putting one foot in front of and above the other, we have to watch where we step, use our hands and and brain in concert with our feet to keep moving and defend ourselves from harm.

As we climb, the view of our Uphill Self is often obstructed. The obstacles seem to shout the same message about your climb:

"We'd rather you didn't!"

These obstacles represent things like physical limitations, inadequate resources, lack of confidence, resistance from people around you who benefit from you staying where you are, competition, health issues, roles and responsibilities, distractions, and poor choices.

We look at a path symbolized by the image above and think, *"well, at least there's a gap between each obstacle where we can rest, recover, and prepare for the next one, right?"*

Certainly the uphill path has its periods of calm -- straightaways where we move up, strengthened by our victory over the previous obstacle and catching our breath as we approach the next one. Places where we can pitch our tents and set up "base camps".

Some will find these good places to level off. They'll look back on the distance they've come, then swivel to gaze at the frightening terrain above and ahead and say, *"You know what? Maybe this is good."* They'll dig a foundation and build a full-on house of brick and mortar, right there in the pleasant meadow of Far Enough, between the skeleton of the vanquished dragon below and the dangerous-looking boulder field above.

That's not you and me.

We might pitch our tents but we're not putting down roots on any slope when there's still a summit ahead. Even when we reach the summit, we know we'll be able to see higher ones from there. Our potential is limitless, and obstacles of increasing difficulty and complexity are the very essence of human life. The principle of *progressive overload* doesn't just build muscles, it operates in the creative and spiritual realms just as well. There are many versions of your Uphill Self, and some can't be seen or imagined until you occupy the space of the version before it.

We don't always get to choose the obstacles on the rise, but here's the master key: **We can choose the slope of the mountain of destiny.**

If you're like me, you were around thirteen years old when you first whined, *"but Mom, I'll never use this algebra and geometry crap in real life!"*

Well, here we are with the most practical and universal of all mathematical applications:

Those tedious lines we had to map out on graph paper in ninth grade? They were all based on this core formula:

Slope = (Change in Y) / (Change in X)

We've already defined our two variables in the images above. X = time, and Y = Identity Delta.

Time or "X" is the easy one. The hash marks between hours, days, years - it's the same for all of us. It's the fixed denominator. The only difference between us are the start and endpoints. My X-axis started in 1966, maybe yours started in 1998. The likelihood of my graph ending before yours is statistically higher but not guaranteed. We just don't know for sure when this dimension of the graph will end for each of us, only that it's limited by our mortality.

The inarguable truth about our X-axis: It's length to the right of NOW is less than it was yesterday, and will be even shorter tomorrow. You can make choices subtracting from it or increase the likelihood of adding a little to it, but you can't multiply this variable beyond the reach of a mortal lifespan.

"Y" or Identity Delta, on the other hand, has a *potentially undefined* upper limit. I say "potentially" because it really depends on what you believe. You are free to impose or perceive limits on yourself at any time:

- Got this disability.
- My family are alcoholics.
- That ship has sailed.
- I'm a victim of trauma.
- I'm not the sharpest tool in the shed.
- My Gerber mixed vegetables weren't served off a silver spoon.

I'm not minimizing the impact or influence of those things. I am saying there is no one who has ever lived who can't make such a list. There is no human life untouched by front-loaded resistance. As bad as you have it, if you search long enough you'll find someone who had it worse yet finished at a higher "Y" level in spite of their situation.

The muscle-bound stick figure in these images does not represent any specific amount of wealth, fame, accomplishment or love. It represents your Uphill Self, a dynamic version of you who has been there, done that, and has an evolved ability to speak what's true and watch it happen on command. You never quite catch him or her, because they are always moving onward and upward, but you can stand in the place they once stood in and be who they once were, on a higher Y-plane than the one you stood on at a previous X-coordinate.

The limitations you accept as *status quo* become *constants* in your slope formula, terminating your life's right triangle at a steepness you're comfortable with.

What are the *variables* on life's Y-axis? Obstacles and effort.

Most linear equations have both variables and constants. The wonderful part is, on the Y-side, you have great agency over determining which is which.

Let me interrupt the program for a moment to recognize how hilarious and poignant it is I'm using math, of all things, as a metaphor for self-development. Math was a great source of pain and tears for me as a teenager, starting with my first ever "D" in 7th grade Pre-Algebra. A lingering stigma of failure in this subject followed me through High School and College. I never really "got it". I saw it as a limitation, a Y-constant keeping me pegged low on life's academic and professional slopes. in retrospect, I realize it was just another obstacle. We've all heard how the human brain continues to develop and grow new neurons intensively until around age 25. I was done with school by that age, and the part of my brain dealing with numbers lagged behind the part in love with words and writing. It was only in my early 30s and discovered the cellular, formula-driven computer spreadsheet that the basics of math came together for me.

So be careful what you label as a constant, when it may simply be a variable with temporary impact on your slope as you advance. It can change as other factors come into play over time and you make choices steepening the grade of your slope.

The next image is designed as a rough representation of the path chosen by someone who desires accelerated growth - a path calculated to stay hot on the heels of one's Uphill Self.

Notice the elements of this image are exactly the same as those in the previous image. Also notice the differences:

- The slope is much steeper.
- The obstacles are concentrated, with little or no space between.
- The amount of time (X) involved is much shorter.
- The amount of Identity Delta (Y) is much greater.
- The overall length of the slope line (distance between current state and goal) is shorter.

You may be thinking, *"WHOA! How am I gonna catch a break on a slope like this? I'll be burned out or eaten for lunch before I get halfway there."*

Relax, you're not necessarily looking at a picture of your entire life. Only a segment of your path, a fragment of the overall mortal linear equation, a sprint in the great journey of life.

It could very well be the picture of a *Five Fearless Days* challenge.

We'll now take a brief detour from this picture, but we'll circle back to it later.

Life Really is a Series of Marathons

Let's switch out of math for a moment and into the world of physical exercise, where a different set of laws apply.

I'm no more an expert in this arena than I am in the world of math, but I know enough to pick out the principles with application in mental and spiritual realms. Those realms comprise what I call personal development.

In Chapter One, I referred to a time in my life when I identified as a distance runner. In my 40s I ran two marathons and many other shorter races. One summer, I ran the same 13 miles every Saturday morning including a very long, steep hill in training for a half marathon. The first few times up the hill, I had to stop running and walk. Eventually I was able to run the whole thing, shaving several minutes off each time. The race I completed in September was a personal best.

One thing I discovered about my body is no matter how carefully I train, and how slowly I approach it, any time I attempt to run more than 20 miles results in an injury. Both marathons wrecked me for weeks afterward. I missed a couple of marathons I had pre-paid for because my twenty-one mile training runs left me limping and unable to run with good form. I learned I lack the genetic gifts allowing me to run more than twenty miles without breaking down physically.

I've long admired the ultra runner Dean Karnazes. He's the guy who ran 50 marathons (26.2 miles each!) in 50 states on 50 consecutive days. If you've never heard of this, you'll be tempted to shake your head and say, "Impossible. He must be some kind of freak of nature!" I won't argue with you. I am physically incapable of emulating Dean's performance, as is nearly everyone reading this. I also know I turned out to be capable of *far more* than I thought possible before I decided to try.

Creative Metabolism

Because science was my second-worst subject after math, let's keep it simple:

Metabolism encompasses all chemical reactions in the body maintaining life. Digestion, breathing, muscle contraction and hormone signaling among others.

"Slow metabolism" is often blamed for weight gain. While it's true not every human being's metabolic rate is the same, lifestyle choices are often the root cause of the variation. If a person has a large amount of stored fat relative to the amount of muscle tissue on their frame, their metabolic capacity will remain limited until certain factors change. When they begin to adjust the ratio by reducing the caloric input resulting in fat storage, specific processes begin to convert the stored fat into energy. This energy is available to fuel processes increasing muscle mass in proportion to the stored fat. Eventually, a more healthy and aesthetic body results.

When Dean Karnazes, the ultra runner, started his 50-day marathon journey, he weighed 154 pounds. When he finished it on day 50, after running over 1,300 miles, he weighed 153 pounds. Surprising? Wouldn't you expect someone subjecting themselves to such an extreme feat of extended endurance to lose a lot more weight?

Here's the difference: Karnazes had honed his metabolism over years of endurance training to the point where no body on earth was more prepared for what he set out to do. Carrying body fat under 5% of his weight (*lean* by any measure), he didn't have much in the way of stored energy. So how did he fuel his insane 50-day marathon streak without breaking down or losing any muscle tissue to speak of?

Food.

With his highly-trained metabolic incinerator on full blast, Karnazes processed 8-10,000 calories per day. Most of us would have a hard time putting away that many calories even with no limits on junk food. We'd get sick and be unable to hold it down. If we did manage to hold it down, we'd get noticeably fatter in a lot less than 50 days.

At different times in my life, I've experienced being lean and having decent metabolic efficiency. I've also experienced times of reduced activity followed by unbalanced metabolism and weight gain.

When I attempted to run more than 20 miles, certain inadequately conditioned or genetically inferior tendons and ligaments began to break down, resulting in injury and forced recovery.

Now, before we become exhausted by this nostalgic side-trip back to junior high school math and science (hey, just be glad I didn't bring up zits and hormones), let's tie it all into your upcoming *Five Fearless Days* challenge.

This book is about finishing a significant and substantial piece of creative work within five days.

Five days of focused work restricted from distractions can be considered and feel like both:

- A sprint in the context of your lifelong creative pursuits, of which these five days will be only a tiny, but highly leveraged fraction.

- A marathon, especially at the beginning of Day One when you're facing many hours in a state you may be unaccustomed to mentally.

Many "healthy" adults aren't runners and make frequent use of escalators, taxicabs and put some effort into finding the parking spot closest to the entrance of their destination building. Not having the necessity or inclination, they haven't really thought about the fact they *haven't actually run* any distance for years.

If you're in this demographic, imagine you're offered $500 to dash 100 meters in 15 seconds. This requires briefly reaching a speed close to 15 miles per hour but is regularly achieved by recreational runners. An untrained person even in their 20s or 30s might be surprised to finish in 18-25 seconds despite their best efforts. Their body is likely to put up tremendous resistance against such an isolated demand and odds of some sort of injury are high.

Likewise if you were offered $10,000 to finish a 26.2-mile marathon within 4 hours without any training, you might be tempted to give it a shot. Within a few miles, you'll encounter signs of physical resistance fatal to your objective. Cramps, side aches, inability to catch your breath. You'll slow down and alternate running with walking, putting the 4-hour finish time out of reach. If you persist, even if your muscles and cardio-respiratory system hold up, underutilized and under-stretched tendons in your hips, knees or feet are likely to fail causing you to develop an asymmetrical gait leading to either an early quit or prolonged agony as your body consumes itself.

In the same way, a creative person who desires to put in the hours and effort resulting in something new and meaningful must be prepared for the sprints and marathons of their work.

We know who the "ultra runners" of the creative world are, because their proven identities are front and center. Steve Jobs, Jeff Bezos, and Elon Musk for business. Stephen King, Charles Dickens and Nora Roberts for writing fiction. Michelangelo and Picasso for outrageous levels of artistic output. They are "household names" for a reason. Read the two statements below and think hard about which holds the most truth about these people:

1. Their work endures because they were brilliant.
2. Their work is brilliant because they endured.

Now consider yourself. Do you identify as an endurance athlete in the area you want to spend these five days working in?

"No, Mike. I'm a serial quitter and I have a hard time sticking with anything for more than fifteen minutes. Why do you think I'm reading your book?"

Hey, just asking.

We're all different. You may be in a place of high confidence and high ability. You've put in some time on the road and can trust your body and mind to keep up. You're reading a book like this because you're always looking for new tools and training tips to take you further. You've got your nose between the right set of pages, so please stay with me. You're the kind of person who gets maximum juice from every squeeze, and we've got the juice.

Others may be standing (or sitting, or lying down) in the sweet spot for a book like this: Openly ambitious creative "couch potatoes" who think of themselves as being in need of some serious help getting off to a solid start. If this is you, take heart: You're not lazy. I'm not patronizing you. I'm simply unwilling to label you because of certain past lazy behaviors leaving you feeling creatively sedentary. You're much better off labeling what you do, then changing it. Who you *are* will follow like a loyal Shih-Tzu.

Every great ultra runner at one point was not one.

Every great writer, artist, sculptor, producer, coder, entrepreneur, composer, dancer and athlete at one time was not. They stared at the blank canvas, white page, empty stage, open market, blinking cursor or heavily-defended field and took a deep, nervous breath. They didn't know any more than you do about what the future held, but they had decided one thing: Quitting was not an option.

The thing they had in common was they chose the path symbolized by the picture on the next page, and rather than back down and take an alternate (there are infinite alternates), they picked up Foot One and put it down on much higher ground than Foot Two stood on. Then they brought Foot Two forward. And so on.

Looking at this picture again, the slope is intimidating. But we're all very familiar with the angle, and unless you've always been physically disabled, you've climbed it a few times simply due to the nature of life.

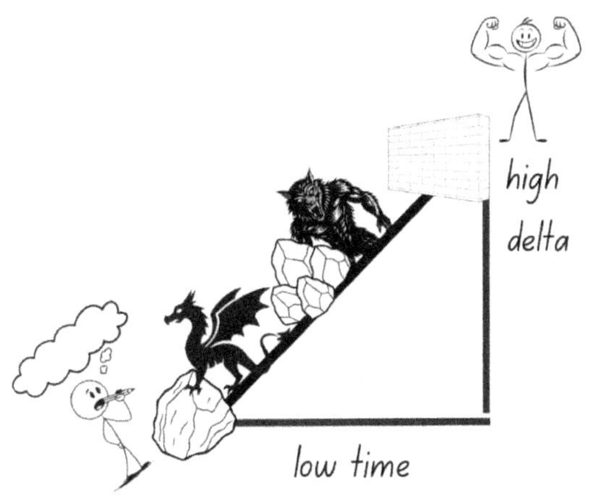

It's basically a 100% grade, a 45-degree angle, a *staircase*. How many actual flights of stairs have you climbed in your life? The path in the picture only resembles one aspect of a staircase, though. You certainly won't get uniform, consistent surfaces on which to place each foot. What you're up against on a high-delta, high-growth slope is closely related to High Intensity Interval Training (HIIT). Climbing a staircase, even an endless one like a Stairmaster, is an aerobic activity. A high-performance, creative life? It will certainly require endurance, but at times it will also require sheer metabolic strength.

The mastery of something as brief as a 25-minute work blocks truly free of all distractions can be the basis of a productive day. Master packing dozens of these into a Five Fearless Days challenge and you'll be setting up the basis of a life of creative achievement.

This chapter was essential for establishing the level of effort required to embark on a five-day challenge. In Chapter Three, we'll dive into the prerequisite decision required. There's no point setting aside five days before knowing exactly what you intend to accomplish with them.

ACTIONS TO COMPLETE BEFORE MOVING ON

❑ Describe here or in a journal entry the aspects of your Uphill Self, a version within your view but separated from you by obstacles you're not quite sure how to overcome.

____

____

____

____

____

____

❑ Describe the obstacles separating you from your Uphill Self:

____

____

____

____

❑ What do you think your Uphill Self would say to you if they had the lines below?

____

____

____

Decide and Commit

The Elements of a Challenge

"Challenge" is the right word.

We hear it in many contexts. What does it really mean?

It has two definitions, both of which apply to our context of *5 Fearless Days:*

1. To invite someone to engage in a contest.
2. To dispute the truth or validity of something.

Let's take on the first definition. Whether it be knights jousting in a medieval tournament, eighteenth-century gentlemen formally defending their honor, or Wild West gunfighters squaring off on a frontier Main Street, the words may be different but the intent was always the same.

"I demand satisfaction, sir!"

"I'll see you in the arena."

"Are you going to pull those guns or whistle dixie?"

The challenge is and always has been a call to action. In bygone days it was freighted with consequences. To accept a challenge was to embrace a fate as dire as death. To back down was to accept defeat by forfeit and public humiliation by association. Lives of challenge losers were cut short and reputations never recovered.

Yes, a five-day challenge is a duel, between the best of you and the worst of you. Not against you and the Uphill Self described in Chapter Two. No. You, the challenger, are up against the Tomorrowist discussed in Chapter One. There will be a winner and a loser. Both are you. You are in a position to rig the contest to the advantage of your champion - The radical Todayist with eyes fixed on the Uphill Self, ready to climb a rugged staircase.

How do you shift the odds in your favor?

It starts with a decision.

Don't mistake a decision for a choice, an option, or a selection.

If you haven't noticed by now, words matter to me. A word's true meaning is like an anchor, and without an anchor you'll drift around the seven seas forever without approaching your intended port.

If *incision* means to cut into something, and *excision* means to cut something out, what do you think *decision* means?

Right - to cut *off* the options you're not going with.

You've heard many phrases and idioms signalling a true decision:

"We're all-in on this now."

"We've scuttled the ships. Let's go."

"It's time to fish or cut bait."

"After much consideration, we're going with Plan A."

"I'll have the chicken piccata, salad on the side."

"Yes! Yes, I will be baptized on June 3rd."

Choices, options and selections are what's spread out in front of you, the near-endless palette of shades and hues available on the paint aisle at Home Depot. The decision is your living room accent wall in "bronzed maple" for the next ten years.

Decisions come in all sizes, from XS to XXXL.

This book isn't about the biggies, except in a tributary way.

A billion dollars, a body of work filling a meter-long shelf, or the fame of a global brand? Those are the Niles, the Yangtzes, and Mississippis of decisions when you consider the volume and flow of time and work required. Honing in on just five days, we're looking at more of the Brown's Creek contribution size. It's all water, it all matters, and it has to flow somewhere.

Your five-day challenge, executed properly, will result in net gain to your life. It cannot result in measurable loss and has very little inherent risk. Five days is what an investor might call a "high leverage" time frame. You have overwhelming odds of getting a lot out of a little time.

In fact, the highest risk involved is choosing not to accept the challenge. That choice is tied to the most significant stakes.

To better understand this exciting situation, consider comparing the best-case and worst-case scenarios:

Scenario Comparison - *Five Fearless Days* Challenge

Worst-Case Scenario:

- You are five days older and nothing is different.

- You have discovered something you don't enjoy doing long enough to stick with for five days.

- You feel disappointed and need to reconsider your larger decisions.

Best-Case Scenario:

- You have a significant breakthrough as a creative person and create a tangible artifact proving it.

- You move the needle measurably toward a larger goal.

- You experience true creative flow over extended time for the first time.

- Your identity as a finisher is strongly reinforced.

- Your confidence expands and you feel empowered to do other things outside the scope of this challenge you felt were beyond you before the challenge.

What do you think? To me, weighing these as "pros and cons" plants taking on the five-day challenge firmly in the "no brainer" category.

It makes me feel like an idiot for not doing it earlier in my life, and I hope you can see why I'm borderline evangelical in my desire to see you commit to it now rather than later.

WHAT-WHEN-WHY-HOW-WHO-WHERE

Let's assume you're with me. You're highly interested in executing *5 Fearless Days*, come what may.

Great. I can almost feel your enthusiasm. But remember, we need a decision, and your decision has prerequisites. We need to focus in on a couple of clarifying questions before we record your decision.

WHY/WHERE/HOW: Don't let these get in the way right now. If you didn't already have a pressure-cooker of a WHY you wouldn't be reading this, and WHERE and HOW are housekeeping items resolved after the decision.

WHO: You, of course. You and me. And whoever else you trust enough to let in on this as an accountability partner. Be ruthlessly selective. More in Chapter Four.

The WHAT: Pin it Down

WHAT: This is a critical element of your decision. What can you do in five days? Put some thought into this. Don't be weak and lame. Come up with something rather unlikely for five days. We tend to wildly underestimate what we can do in a dedicated block of time because, well, we're not used to dedicating time. We're used to weaving the threads of creative work into the fabric of our busy days, and often those threads are the first to be skipped when we're tired or overwhelmed. Not allowed here. Your challenge moves your objective into the Priority One position for five consecutive days.

Odds are, you already know exactly what you'd like to do with your five days. If not, there are two main categories to consider:

1. Creation/Production
2. Skill acquisition

Creation/production options include all forms of creation, using skills and talents you possess and want to expand and develop.

Skill acquisition includes learning "how to do" any number of things. Tight structure should be built around a challenge like this. For example, reading Stephen Covey's *7 Habits of Highly Effective People* is indisputably a good idea, but simply "reading" it won't do you much more good than reading the latest *Jack Reacher* novel. A paid interactive course built around the *7 Habits* with assignments, deadlines and written action plans takes it to the challenge level. For a complete newbie aspiring coder, avoid a challenge objective like "learn Python" and go with something like "code three simple, functional Python apps" instead.

What can you do in five days without distractions? This objective should have at least one number (pages, modules, chapters, posts, units, dollars, etc.).

Some one-line specific examples:

- Outline and draft 10 Medium articles in the RC airplane niche, with photography.

- First draft five chapters of my book *Changing Lanes: Career Transition after 40.*

- Create a sculpture titled *Another Man's Treasure* from the junk in my garage.

- Learn enough ChatGPT to create 5 useful custom GPTs to share with co-workers.
- Write music and lyrics for five new songs on acoustic guitar.

Go Stretch or Go Home

Some cortisol and a little adrenaline should be present as you write this out for the first time. This isn't fear. Don't label it as such or listen to any voice trying to apply such a label. It's anticipation. Trepidation. A healthy spike of nerves indicating you're breaking new ground. Embrace it.

If it doesn't cause you to pause with pen in hand, wondering if you just might be biting off slightly more than can be comfortably chewed, you're not thinking big enough. My experience is most people should add another 20% for good measure, and they usually meet or beat the stretch due to the "flow bonus".

You sense the blank space coming up. At this point, you can see it.

It's time.

You've only got one line. If it takes more, it's too complicated. Write it now.

MY FIVE FEARLESS DAYS OBJECTIVE:

____

You've just made half of a decision. Don't freak out - it's not carved in stone. You're a free agent and you can revise, expand, or reduce as much as your instinct and wisdom prompt you to, right up until the time you're in the arena.

IMPORTANT: Your challenge objective should contain no dependencies on what other people do. *5 Fearless Days* is meant for solo efforts – things you can do on your own. The objective to "sell ten widgets" doesn't work because it depends on ten people deciding to buy your widget. "Make 30 sales presentations" doesn't work either because your prospects must decide to show up. This doesn't mean a sales-related objective is off-limits, but you'd need to get down to something like "make 100 sales calls" to eliminate dependencies on anything but your own efforts.

The WHEN: The Other Half of the Decision

This one will prevent 90% of those who read this book from using it for anything more than entertainment.

(A friend visiting your place sees 5 Fearless Days on your shelf)

"Hey, I heard about this book. Is it any good?"

"Oh, that book? Um, yeah. It's a good one."

"Cool. So you did the five-day challenge?"

"What, who me? No. Not yet."

(Friend happens to be the smart, brutally honest and genuinely helpful type who could make a great Accountability Partner)

"Then why are you telling me it's good?"

If you don't plan and schedule your first five-day challenge *before you finish reading this book,* or even this *chapter,* your likelihood of experiencing its benefits drops off the chart.

Is the incorrigible Tomorrowist whispering sweet *somedays* into your ear right now?

Shake it off. Let's schedule this thing right now.

Get out your calendar.

Working 8-5 on salary and only get 15 days off per year? Cough it up. What matters more - five days of sunburn and pricey drinks in the Bahamas, a five-season re-binge of *Stranger Things* or the fulfillment of your potential as a human being?

If your answer's not the third choice, stuff like the the first two will dominate your life's highlight reel, and your colorful Instagram stories will be your legacy. Okay with that? Fine, let this book be kindling for the flames taking your childhood dreams up in smoke.

Maybe you can extend a 3-day holiday weekend by a couple of days. Get creative. It might be a few weeks before you can pull it off. Just block it off with intention.

How far away do these five days need to be?

I strongly suggest a time frame of **between ten and thirty days from the time you finish reading this book for the first time,** for reasons more fully explained in Chapter Five. For your own reasons, you may need longer, and if so, be prepared to review this book again and follow a 30-day lead-up training program to your challenge. If you feel ready to start in as few as ten days, a full program is outlined in Chapter Five. If it looks like it'll be 30+ days, start at T-minus 30 days with the full program outlined in the Appendix.

How clear do these five days need to be?

As clear as you're willing and able to make them.

You may have kids to dress and get to school or day care, and you have no backup to take over those responsibilities. People who look to you for food preparation, transportation, and general attention. Use discretion and discernment to simplify, delegate, and set expectations.

Despite your best intentions, you may not be in a place where you can ethically go full "monk mode" and disappear without a trace for five days. But you can make arrangements to deposit the majority of your waking hours into an account you can draw from. It may require foresight, creativity, and a little firmness.

You can do this.

Got your five days set aside? Grab an instrument of writing and list the actual dates right here.

MY FIVE FEARLESS DAYS (DATES):

DAY ONE_______________________________________

DAY TWO_______________________________________

DAY THREE_____________________________________

DAY FOUR______________________________________

DAY FIVE_______________________________________

Congratulations. You've already done more than most do. *If* you actually wrote your goal and those dates down.

Turn back a couple of pages. Did you write out both your objective and the dates? Because if you just skipped over it thinking *"I'll do it later"* or *"I'm too lazy to find a pen right now"*, or *"this is a freakin' ebook!"*, you have listened to and obeyed the deceitful Tomorrowist. The odds of this book doing you a lick of good just got cut in half, and that's a generous estimate. (eBook readers: Get some paper!)

Look, I've been the kind of person who gets annoyed when an author asks me to actually do something. The kind of reader who soaks it all in and lets it "marinate" my timid little ambitions in the hopes they'd catch fire and start cooking on their own. I'd flip through books in the bookstore, and if there were blanks I was supposed to fill out, it'd go right back on the shelf. *Writing in a book? Kinda blasphemous, isn't it? I buy books to read, not to be handed assignments like a seventh-grader. Right?*

In retrospect, I was a rather dim bulb in the chandelier of readers.

The genre we're in here is called Self-Help. Personal Development. Which authors do you think are going to facilitate you helping yourself or developing as a person? The ones who impress you with their academic research and stately paragraphs, or the ones who demand you not only think in response but take action?

I'm lowering the lance of this imperative on the authority of experience: Write it down. On a separate journal or sheet of paper if necessary.

We good? Great. Let's move on.

Go Fearless. Even If You Feel Fear.

Look at the cover of this book for a second. The title: *5 Fearless Days*.

Why do you think I chose the word *fearless* as a descriptive modifier for your chosen days? (besides the pretty alliteration of the f's)

Because there's nothing to fear.

Can you die doing this? Will you be horribly maimed or traumatized? What exactly do you have to lose?

It's just not a long enough frame of time for you to be afraid of.

Now, imagine the title *90 Fearless Days* or *365 Fearless Days*. Someone might have the guts to write those books, but it won't be me. Anyone who claims they can get you through so much time without experiencing some some serious fear is selling you something they don't own.

We'll keep a hard focus on our five days.

Yes, life goes on afterward. Yes, it may be months before you get another five-day stretch like this.

But there's no reason to wallow in terror during the 120 measly hours of this challenge. Your biggest fear should be what happens if you *don't* take any action at all, because this choice (and it is a choice) is the only one carryuing any real potential for negative consequences.

The choice to carry on as usual *after learning what you could do* carries the highest odds of feeling emotions related to failure, inadequacy and loss of confidence. Those things are scary.

So when you consider *not* starting with a five-day challenge leading to significantly bigger and better things, you have my permission to be terrified. Why shouldn't abandoned or delayed human potential have the face of Pennywise the Clown, Dr. Frankenstein's patchwork man or Count Orlok? You know, neither alive nor dead and something you should definitely run from?

C'mon Mike, I don't need your challenge. I can just "weave" my creative work into my life as part of a bespoke daily routine. I just need to do a little bit every day. I'll get it done without your drastic measures of carving five whole days outta my crazy life.

Yeah. Kind of like you've already been getting it done, right?

This chapter is designed to persuade you to set aside five specific days in the near future to focus on something meaningful to you.

If I've accomplished that mission, you're ready to turn over a new leaf.

A new leaf is symbolized by the next page, which you're about to turn over into Chapter Four.

This is where we burn the bridges, scuttle the ships, and stop looking back.

Please don't go until you can check the list below 100% with confidence:

ACTIONS TO COMPLETE BEFORE MOVING ON:

- ❑ Write down your five-day objective, and make it a little bigger than you think can be done.
- ❑ Select the specific days and dates of your challenge and write them in this book and in whatever calendar you use.
- ❑ Set down this book, stand up, nod your head twice and say out loud, "Yes! I'm DOING this!"

The Binding

Time and the Elements of a Challenge

Comedian Brian Regan has a routine in which he ridicules the very idea of directions on a box of Pop-Tarts. He mimes holding the box and shouts with bulged eyes in his self-deprecating idiot voice, *"How do I get that goodness in me?"* Then he turns the "box" and reads:

1. Toast the Pop-Tarts
2. Go ahead, toast 'em.
3. Hey, are you still reading this?

For too long, I looked at self-development books, videos and podcasts like Regan's box of Pop-Tarts: If I read, watch and listen long enough, I'll "get that goodness in me" and start doing amazing things.

I should've just skipped straight to: "Go ahead, toast 'em."

We tend to spend a lot of time in the "great unready" portion of our lives, seeing past the current obstacle into the promised land, a perpetually moving target.

"Got college first."

"Got this job. Might take me a couple years of head-down hard-driving to get there."

"Had a baby. Probably won't sleep for the next year or so."

"Look, I'm 25. Even if it takes me three years, I can still start when I'm 27 and have it done by 30."

Youth is a double-edged sword. Someone in their early 20's has a perspective of time appearing limitless and open-ended. So many years ahead, you can't count the decades on the fingers of one hand. The number of days? It's in the tens of thousands. Surely you're entitled to YOLO a couple thousand on feel-good entertainments.

One in their 50's, on the other hand, reaches an internal tipping point where one makes peace with the fact there are more days behind than ahead. The number of those days is less certain, especially considering the random, intermittent jolts of pain in one's abdomen or the refusal of one's knee joint to bend properly.

Time, the abundant asset the young person was willing to exchange in truckloads for money, becomes a precious commodity the aging person would gladly exchange their accumulated wealth for.

What if you, as a not-so-old person, could leverage the graybeard's wisdom regarding time?

This is what *5 Fearless Days* is all about.

A successful five days is nearly a foregone conclusion where these elements are present:

1. A specific DECISION
2. A specific COMMITMENT
3. A specific PLAN for each day

4. Assigned ACCOUNTABILITY

5. A specific REWARD for completion

You've already fulfilled the first element with your writing on the previous pages. If you haven't yet done the writing, I invite you to pause and experience burning shame for about ten seconds.

Now, take a deep breath and say out loud, *"Life is not a spectator sport. This is the last time I'll be dishonest with myself about this."*

Now do the writing. Go ahead, we'll wait.

Back?

Good, let's go. My apologies to those who did it the first time and have to sit through this digression. I promise this is the last time. Some people need a little more coaching than others and this is a "no-reader-left-behind" sort of book.

The Elements of Your Decision

You have established your choices of **what** and by **when.**

Together, these comprise a decision.

During these five days you've decided (cut off the options) you won't be on a cruise, watching Hulu, hiking the Adirondacks, carousing drunkenly with friends or climbing the slippery rungs of someone else's corporate ladder.

You've also decided exactly what you WILL do during those five days, and you may already be feeling like you've bitten off a bigger hunk of pine sap than you bargained for.

Ponderous thought-bubbles containing negativity bombs detonate in the air around your head even as dozens of butterfly wings bump against your stomach lining:

"I've never done this much in five days before."

"Maybe I should wait until after (insert whatever your eloquent Tomorrowist comes up with)."

"My family's not going to let me do this."

"Why did I even pick up this stupid book?"

These thoughts are good signs. They are evidences you've made a real decision. You're right where you want to be. Your spectacularly evolved brain is performing a service it was designed for over hundreds of generations.

In the timeline of *homo sapiens*, it wasn't that long ago when behavior divergent from what everyone else was doing got you dismembered or killed in short order. For example, if the clan rule was "we lock the cave door an hour after sunset", there were reasons behind it. Those who enjoyed midnight stargazing while strolling the savanna unarmed became cul-de-sacs of the gene pool as they fell prey to hungry predators with teeth, claws, and superior night vision.

Today, not so much. Civilization has changed our lives in dramatic ways, but our brains remain virtually unchanged.

We still have laws backed by protective reason. We should keep those laws for the societal good of all. But there are other rules we've internalized with little bearing on our safety, some of which only hold us in long-term patterns of mediocrity and stunted growth.

A five-day challenge focused on your highest creative calling is a strong move against the drive to homeostasis, the source of negative energy fueling your "stuck" feeling.

It's a breakout. If you follow your decision with the other elements, it's a potential *breakthrough*.

Your Contract: Put it in Writing

Next comes COMMITMENT. While your decision marks a line in the sand from which there should be no turning back, commitment shifts new energy into the part of your life lying ahead of your decision in time.

This shift in energy and paradigm is supercharged by a contract.

The most basic definition of a contract is "a legally binding agreement between two or more parties." In essence, the agreement you're about to make holds the following **three parties** accountable for the stated result:

1. The "You" who has not yet done what you want to do.
2. The "You" who has already mastered the skill of finishing stated commitments and doesn't quit on them.
3. One or more interested and honest Accountability Partners.

Since the first two parties both reside within the walls of your own epidermis, it won't be necessary to introduce them. You're not negotiating with yourself. You are taking instruction from a part of you who has already done what you're about to do.

The third-party role of Accountability Partner (AP) should be filled by a person in possession of a very particular set of skills (think Liam Neeson in *Taken)* and should be recruited with care and consideration.

It's action time again.

Acquire a pristine sheet of paper. The blankest, whitest one you can find. I thought about putting the contract template right here in the book but this document needs its own space.

Write "CONTRACT" at the top, and make it bold. A Sharpie would not be out-of-scope for this word. If you have a calligraphic fountain pen and know how to use it, this is the ultimate use case. If you don't see this as serious business, you won't take it seriously.

Next, below CONTRACT and using smaller but no less intentional print, write "I, (insert your full legal name), hereby commit to (insert your five-day challenge objective) by midnight on (insert the last date of your challenge).

Below that, write in bold capitals "ATTESTATION AND CERTIFICATION", with the following text below it (yes, verbatim) with a legibility your nearsighted grandmother would thank you for:

On my honor, I hereby commit to and promise to start and finish what is documented herein. I fail to do do so at peril of my internal sense of integrity and self-confidence. Any temporary lapse will be immediately acknowledged. I will forgive myself and resume a consistent practice. At stake is my identity as a professional who follows-through on commitments regardless of distraction and resistance. I hereby promise to follow the instructions given by my guide and communicate with total integrity with my accountability partner(s). I will not sleep until the day's assigned work is done.

Sign your full name below this with solemn formality and any epic flourishes defining your personality.

Below your signature, write "Witness and Accountability Partner:" and leave a space for their signature.

So who is this mysterious person who will read and sign your contract under your name?

Your AP: Your Mom Need Not Apply

Choose wisely. It could be your spouse, partner, brother, sister, cousin, friend, or anyone who really cares about you. Except your mom. Unless she is notorious for her tough love and you respond to it, moms tend to let their offspring off too easy. As do at least 80% of "nice" friends.

A qualified AP has the following characteristics:

- They know the details of and support your decision.
- They care about you as a person and want to see you succeed.
- They will not hesitate to immediately call you out on contract violations.
- They value honesty and forthrightness over compassion and protection of your feelings.
- They are the kind of person you admire for doing something similar to what you are setting out to do - someone standing up there next to your Uphill Self.

- They can be trusted to proactively check in with you daily before, during and after your challenge without your reaching out to them.

If an AP has to be reminded of their duties, you've chosen the wrong person. This must be someone you are willing to show your work to, someone who will take a few minutes to confirm you've done it.

Your AP has no responsibility to read, review, beta-test, critique or praise any aspect of your work except the *doneness* of it (or lack thereof). They are literally there to "keep you honest". If you don't respect them and feel an impulse to make them proud, you've chosen poorly. If they think the job of AP is to "spare your feelings" and make you feel good about yourself, they are worse than useless in this role.

Here's what the voice of a legit AP might sound like:

"Your goal was ten pages today and you got eleven? Spectacular. I knew you could do it. Ten more tomorrow, I'm looking forward to talking about it. You're on a roll - keep the momentum up."

Or, *"What the hell? You only got nine pages out of ten? I'm extremely disappointed. Really, you're letting one page violate our contract? My name is on that thing. Let's add your shortfall to tomorrow's goal. I do not want to be a witness to a train wreck, certainly not by one stupid page. Come on."*

You need to have the guts to find these people and make it crystal clear what their responsibilities are, and you expect nothing less. Finding the right AP is a clear signal you mean business.

Odds are, as you read over the characteristics of the ideal AP, one or more people come to mind. If you have two strong candidates, try to recruit them both. If you just can't think of anyone, you may need to emerge from your shell a bit more. You may find the perfect AP among people you've had some friendly engagement with on social media. In particular, anyone who has offered constructive feedback on your work.

I have personally filled the role of AP for people of people between the ages of 18 and 64 in five different countries. If you need an AP who knows exactly what the *5 Fearless Days* challenge is all about and want to swap AP duties for each other, you can sign up for a cohort for specific challenge dates at 5FearlessDays.com.

Once your AP(s) have reviewed and signed your contract, the document is complete. It's now binding. Respect it.

So why the contract? We're all adults here. Why can't you just read the book and keep your commitments in your head? You know, like a DIY thing?

Look, I've read all the inspiring and repetitive social media posts telling us to "disappear, and come back unrecognizable" and how you should do your work in secret to protect it from discouraging input and "tell nobody" until you suddenly unleash your fabulous work upon an unsuspecting world.

Then there's the other side of this advice, which is to "build in public" and post everything you do in real time, exposing it to the comments of everyone from vitriolic meme trolls to your mom - requiring you respond to all this feedback and deal with the emotions it stirs up instead of getting your work done.

Both sets of advice are bad in isolation, and contribute to the blockages and "stuckness" leading you to this book.

In my experience, the happy medium is to do your work within sight of a tight, carefully selected circle of high-quality humans. A handful you know, trust, and who care about you. They don't need to be "into" your genre or whatever you're creating, and you don't need their feedback on anything except the volume of your output and how it measures up to your commitment. They're just people who are delighted you're moving forward with what you really love doing and aren't afraid to call you on the carpet for not doing what you promised you would do.

Honesty: Much More Than a Policy

Here's what you should internalize as you draw up your contract and recruit your APs: The five-day challenge is not about "doing better" or "doing more". In the long run, you gain little by writing 37 pages when your contract was for 50 and saying "welp, better than nothing, sure glad I did this challenge!"

No.

Any outcome short of commitment is failure. Believing anything less guarantees mediocrity. It undercuts your cause and downgrades your self-confidence.

Such a belief normalizes dishonesty.

Those aren't pretty verbs, my friend, and there's no nicer way to put it.

This might be a worse result than if you abandon your contract after a few hours to rip open open a party-sized bag of Cheetos paired with a quart of Ben & Jerry's to "be good to yourself" and forget this mean book.

Come on, Mike. That's harsh. *Something* is always better than nothing.

Is it, now?

is it truly better to train yourself to settle for "less than" and "good enough" and "whatever" on an increasingly vague and sliding scale, and admit you're not a self-starter? To enjoy life as it gets served to you by attention-scavenging algorithms?

Remember how aggravating it was in school figuring out how teachers graded your academic performance? Math and science were easy -- Numbers don't lie, and there's only one right answer.

Then there was reading comprehension and literature.

The closest corollary to our five-day challenge is the English teacher's most basic assignment: "Write a 500-word essay on..." As kids, we heard one thing and latched onto it: 500 words. Remember counting them? Remember running out of things to say on the topic at 243 words? Remember developing skills such as bloat, plagiarism, repetition and even speculative fiction to make up the difference?

The teacher was after more than a number. Your random stream of consciousness about your cocker spaniel clocking in at 501 words wasn't going to get you a passing grade, let alone extra credit. Because the assignment was to write about Anne Frank's *Diary of a Young Girl.*

As we matured and moved into the upper grades and even university, we learned to show up with more balance between quantity and quality. The word count was simply a guide to the volume of the content, and the meaning of the content is what mattered.

But your grade *would* still be docked if you didn't meet the word count.

So it is with the five-day challenge.

The last thing you want as an adult creative is to train yourself to believe 74% of done is "good".

Need I remind you this is a C- in a standard grading matrix?

It's Not About Perfectionism, So Dismount Your High-Horse

Please don't accuse me of being a "perfectionist" or triggering you by demanding you be one. There is a big difference between "perfection" of output and precision in keeping a contract commitment, which is well within the range of average human capability.

5 Fearless Days is "first draft" territory. Whatever it is you're making, it's not the time to perfect it, put the finishing touches on it, and ship it, unless it's a small project and you can complete all required steps within the five-day frame.

So focus on getting your "500 words" (insert your actual numerical goal for completion within 5 days), without worrying too much about how "good" it is. You're a grown-up now. You're not going to fill your draft with *lorem ipsum* nonsense. You're going to do your best work without polishing, obsessing over details, editing or self-criticism. That comes later.

With bigger projects, the scope of your challenge is to create a specific body of raw material from which the polished product will later emerge. **The act of getting as far as your commitment, even if it turns out to be more work than you expected, is vital to the meeting of future deadlines.** There will be plenty of those.

This small challenge is essential training for bigger ones.

If we compare your five-day project to Michelangelo's masterpiece *David*, you're not trying to sculpt the veins in David's biceps or the individual hairs in his eyebrows. In five days you've committed to having the form of a young man revealed from a slab of marble with a head, shoulders, torso, legs and feet. If instead your marble more closely resembles a hippopotamus after five days, you've fallen short, and your AP should rightfully shake their head in disgust.

This is really about honesty.

A proven ability to do precisely what you committed to do is a wildly underestimated superpower. It is the wellspring of creative prolificity. Think about it - If you've persuaded yourself with repeated experiences ***what you say you'll do invariably gets done***, what exactly can stop you within the limits of time and mortality?

To make this point, let's consider the ultimate example: I believe God created and maintains the universe by the power of His integrity. We know from multiple references in the Bible He cannot lie. When he shouts "Let there be light" into the void, light has no option but to respond. The power to have work done, then, is an expression of honesty.

A Word (okay, 583 words) on Motivation: Your Reward

There are books on the topic of motivation thicker than five copies of *Five Fearless Days* stacked, annotated and supported by a vast body of scientific research. It's beyond our scope. If you weren't motivated, why would you be reading this?

Motivation can be classified as *intrinsic* and *extrinsic*.

Intrinsic motivation for your five-day challenge lies in the work itself. I talk about the elements of work-based intrinsic motivation with the acronym TSA (apologies to the oft-maligned yet unfortunately essential government agency):

Talent: You are driven by a knack for or at least an inclination toward this kind of work, and feel positive internal pressure to get progressively better at it.

Service: You are moved to act knowing your finished work will be of value to and useful for someone other than yourself. This includes those within your sphere who potentially are fed, clothed and housed by the proceeds of your effort.

Agency: Of all the things you could choose to do with your five days, you choose this because it brings you joy. It completes an aspect of you.

Where TSA is present, things tend to get done. In the absence of one or more of its elements drift, confusion and goal-abandonment are likely.

Extrinsic motivation, on the other hand, is a pressure from outside yourself taking many forms, some more urgent than others:

- Need $2,000 by the 25th or I'm homeless again.
- A million in the bank is an important milestone to me.
- I'm gonna let myself snarf 4 whole Ding-Dongs once I finish this.
- The LED countdown timer wired to these explosives must be addressed.

For the context of our five-day challenge, we're going to set aside both the long game and any life-or-death drama. You'll augment the primary power of intrinsic motivation (TSA) by stacking it with a simple extrinsic factor rooted in delayed gratification.

Choose something simple - something you would eventually do or buy for yourself anyway. Something spiking dopamine in your brain just thinking about it - and make it a condition of your fulfilled contract.

For example, say you enjoy visiting a beloved Indian restaurant every couple of weeks for a *Tikka Masala* you can't stop raving about. For you, sitting down to warm curry amid the spicy smells from the kitchen, the exotic decor and friendly service is the perfect kickoff to a weekend. Going to this special place and enjoying the sensory experience of the meal is rewarding for you.

Schedule your next visit for dinner the night of Day Five of your challenge. But here's the kicker: *You don't get to go if you fail to fulfill or exceed the terms of your contract.* Period. No soup for you. You stay home and ponder your life choices over microwaved leftover meatloaf or a bowl of Shredded Wheat.

One early *5 Fearless Days* challenger told me the reward she'd set was the purchase of a specific model of vacuum cleaner. As her AP for the challenge, I thought this was pretty funny at the time, but I'm smarter now. She associates positive feelings with cleaning her carpet. She had plans to buy a new one soon anyway. Who am I to judge?

It's different for everyone. You may be in the habit of treating yourself to a new article of clothing every payday. A movie and popcorn with friends. A few hours with a mystery novel on a Sunday afternoon. Simple pleasures of consumption empty of TSA in themselves but with power to move you. The difference is, you can wisely use them as tools contributing to a growing body of finished work.

Fearless Hack: Use smaller blocks of high-dopamine entertainment as rewards for larger blocks of creative completion, not as escape from boredom.

The worst trap you can set for yourself is a reward for quitting. Repeat this more than once and your subconscious will quickly realize *"hey, if it gets too hard I can always bail and go do something that feels better."* Before you know it, you're moping around whimpering, *"I'm just not the kind of person who finishes things"* like it's some sort of birthright. Instead, tie all rewards to the back end of DONE and don't hesitate to deny yourself the prize if you fall short, even by 1%.

Bottom line: This skill (and it is a skill anyone can develop to whatever degree they want) separates those who get it done from those who don't.

In Chapter Five, we'll focus on the "training days" leading up to your five-day challenge and specific steps you can take to guarantee success. But first, please take care of the essential housekeeping items below.

ACTIONS TO COMPLETE BEFORE MOVING ON:

❑   Review the five elements of a successful five-day challenge.

❑   Write up and sign your CONTRACT.

❑   Recruit and set expectations with your Accountability Partner(s) and have them undersign your name on the contract.

❑   Complete the following prompt here or in your journal: "Honesty in fulfilling the terms of my contract is important because:

____

____

____

____

❑   Describe the TSA of the motivation behind your challenge. What is your talent? Who will your work serve? Why do you choose this over everything else?

____

____

❑   What is the simple reward you'll treat yourself to after a finished contract, one you're willing to deny yourself in the event of falling short?

Preparing For Your Challenge

Take a look at your calendar. How many days are there between now and Day One of your *5 Fearless Days*?

In Chapter Three I recommended a time frame of ten to thirty days between the day you sign your contract and the first calendar day of your challenge. Why? Isn't this procrastination? Wouldn't it be best to just jump into it tomorrow morning with a loud "Let's go!"?

Love the attitude, but no.

This requires preparation. There are dangers in not having enough prep time as well as having too much. It's important to understand both in order to design an effective training program as your five-day sprint approaches.

"I Wasn't Ready": Not Enough Time

You've heard of smokers, drinkers, or drug users going "cold turkey" in an effort to quit their habit. Maybe you've even experienced such a thing yourself. Not pleasant. Results are mixed. For every success story you hear, there'll be three others of almost immediate relapse.

Face facts - your brain is addicted to certain things. The most obvious is the circus of pixels dancing across high-resolution screens around your house and in your pocket. If what you see and hear on these devices isn't sufficiently entertaining, you're conditioned to expend a tenth of a calorie to flick your finger or press a button causing the scene to shift instantly. Algorithms lurking in acres of water-cooled data centers track your flicks and serve up more of what you linger on, peppered with ads. It's as if the mad scientists in your unfriendly neighborhood meth lab relentlessly tweak their recipe to find the ingredients making you forget life had any purpose beyond gawking and flipping interrupted by occasional impulse buying.

So now, suddenly, you're going to sit down for five full days of waking hours with your phone in another room and nothing but a blank page, a blinking cursor, or an empty canvas in front of you?

Wait, did he just say 'phone in another room'?

Yes he did.

If you think you're going to get anything worthwhile done in 120 hours with your digital Pez dispenser lit up by your side with random notifications spamming your face, you're delusional. A *5 Fearless Days* Challenge cuts the umbilical, turns off the mainline and pushes you into a corner with a demand to produce. Anything less is half-baked, off the reservation and doomed to failure.

Ten days is the absolute rock-bottom minimum time frame required to prepare *unless* you can check ALL of these boxes honestly without hesitation:

- ❑ You can easily go 3-4 hours during the day without looking at your phone.
- ❑ You don't have any push notifications enabled from social media platforms.

- ❑ You watch less than three movies or TV show episodes per month.
- ❑ You regularly do things like walk a mile, wash dishes or fold laundry without any TV, podcasts or music on.
- ❑ Outside of your "day job", you complete at least 3-5 focused blocks of 45-60 minutes per week.
- ❑ You can easily stand in line for ten minutes without reaching for your phone or grinding your teeth.

If you quickly checked all boxes, take a bow: You are one buff challenger. Do not pass go and proceed directly to Chapter Six.

Checked few or none? Don't feel bad. There are few who can. Hence the rest of this chapter and this entire book.

Intent Decay: Waiting Too Long

At the other extreme is the problem of having too many days between now and your challenge.

The primary risk of a long intervening time frame between decision and inception is *intent decay*. Salespeople are very familiar with this psychological concept, which means the emotions making a purchase likely in the beginning slowly fade in intensity as time passes. If an attempt to consummate the sale is not made early, the opportunity may be lost after the prospect "sleeps on it".

So even though you've fully bought into the concept of *5 Fearless Days*, you risk it becoming an afterthought by inserting more than a month between now and your start date.

Maybe this book gets set aside as something else on your reading list takes its place on the nightstand. Mountains of new content queue up to pile into your brain, displacing and minimizing concepts and commitments picked up in these pages. Your original signed Contract document may wind up folded and wedged between pages, forgotten. If you've scheduled time off from work, your brain starts scanning for other things to do with the time that don't feel so spartan. Some friends invite you to join them for a road trip to Yellowstone. A vigilant algorithm scrapes your reserved days off your device and serves you up an ad for 50% off a Caribbean cruise on the same dates.

Without specific actions designed to keep you locked in on your original intention, your intention could erode even within the "training zone" of 10-30 days.

Cue the Montage: Your *5 Fearless Days* Training Program

In the classic 1976 film *Rocky*, a small-time boxer who just got kicked out of his locker at the local gym for being a "bum" is offered the chance of a lifetime - to fight the world heavyweight champ in an exhibition bout. Foremost among the obstacles Rocky Balboa faces is time: He gets the offer the day before Thanksgiving for a fight scheduled for New Year's Day. Since he's been working as a small-time debt collector for a local loan shark, he's not in the best shape. His first morning run culminates in a staggering ascent of the steps of the Philadelphia Museum of Art leaving him doubled over, gasping for breath.

That's Point A.

Then something remarkable in cinema history happens. Bill Conti's iconic theme "Gonna Fly Now" becomes the soundtrack with other sounds and dialogue muted. Our hero jogs through the streets of his hometown and sprints the length of a large ship along the dock. He performs one-armed push-ups under the watchful eye of his manager. He attacks frozen sides of beef in the local meat-packing plant with a barrage of bare, bloody fists. And finally, he takes those steps again, three or four at a time, arriving at the top with enough energy to turn and face the city with arms raised in triumph. The passage of five weeks between Thanksgiving and the end of the year is implied and summarized as we see Rocky grow in strength and endurance right before our eyes.

In just 3.5 minutes of movie time, we arrive at Point B.

Sure, these montages have become Hollywood cliches. The audience has no time for every tedious rep, 5am chugging of raw eggs, and all the setbacks and recoveries involved in a protagonist's actual preparations for conflict. They're happy to receive the message "Look, the hero worked his butt off over the next five weeks and transformed himself. You get it, right? Enjoy these highlights with cool music on the side."

You must create your own montage.

But you don't get to watch. You're in the underdog role. The central protagonist is you *en route* to your Uphill Self, and you live every minute of it.

Your routine is not about churning arms and legs, speed bags and barbells. Although your physical condition is extremely important to anything you do in life, the content supporting those transformations can be found elsewhere. I trust you to find it.

The exercises required to build the stamina required for your five-day challenge are all about boredom, quiet, stillness, delay, and sacrifice.

Hollywood has no interest in scripts like this.

But if you buy this script, you'll unlock the potential to achievements withheld from you in the past because you have not been the person capable of achieving them.

Building Your Training Program

Remember the image at the top of the next page. It can represent your five-day challenge, your ten-to-thirty-day preparation montage, your larger project, or your entire life. The point of the picture is *you choose steep*. You desire high delta in short time, whatever the time frame and target. As the slope steepens, the rocks and monsters slide down toward you and you willingly take them on with little to no "messing around" between. The whole idea is to get better, faster.

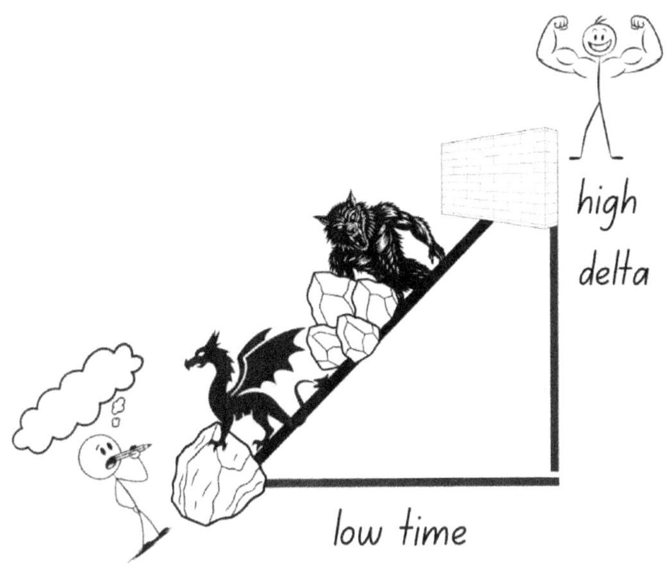

Don't interpret this image to imply there's no rest between obstacles. **High-intensity focus requires high-quality recovery**. But remember, you're pitching tents, not building castles. Your resting points are base camps, not homesteads.

As mentioned earlier in this chapter, some challengers may be more prepared for their challenge than others. Some may already be highly-disciplined, free of hampering addictions and ready to start tomorrow.

Others, not so much. You may feel like you're living a double life, torn between your "job" and your creative identity. Your day job is your bill-paying Sugar Daddy so it gets most of your energy. Evenings and weekends feel like well-deserved R&R time, and you find yourself taking refuge in sports, movies, shows, food, drink, and socializing. Because heck, everyone else is doing those things. Sure, you feel a pull to a higher calling, so you read good books like this, too. You listen to great podcasts during walks, runs, and tedious chores. You throw enough bones to your Uphill Self to keep the other voice out of your face while you wander off into sideshows.

Wherever you are along this continuum, and however many days you have until Day One, you'll need to leverage those days to increase four core capacities:

1. Attention Stamina

You may have the attention span of a gnat. You weren't born this way. This has been trained into you, and it can be trained out using the same principles.

2. Boredom Tolerance

Modern digital life has conditioned you to expect something colorful, funny and new every few seconds. Your five-day challenge requires you to sit with discomfort, repetition and blank slates for hours at a time. If you're not ready for this, you'll be overwhelmed by a quit impulse.

3. Deep Rest Capacity

When you're done with work, you're done. Close the book, shut it down. Reward yourself precisely with exactly what you promised yourself and no more. You will train yourself to crave the return to work, not the escape at the end of it. Otherwise, your *5 Fearless Days* will turn into five sleepy, exhausted days.

4. Dealing with Device Separation

It's hard to believe full internet access wasn't available on phones until 2007. Whatever did people do before? For those who can't remember, we got a lot more done. You'll go old-school and learn to deal without your phone in the same way people get over their fear of spiders: Gradual exposure.

This chapter contains a 10-day program covering the minimum run-up to a five-day challenge. You can find a longer version covering the 30-day time frame complete with checklists and mindset scripts in the Appendix.

The 10-Day Pre-Challenge Training Program

NOTE: The "work" you do during your training program as challenge prep can be related to your challenge contract, but it's not required. You can even leverage your job for the first few days of your challenge training. For this to work, you need to be able to truly work in "do not disturb" mode for up to 60 minutes at a time. Make sure your colleagues and leaders understand what you're asking for so you don't come across as willfully unresponsive: Undisturbed blocks of time to get more work done faster. No one needs to know what you're planning to do on your upcoming days off. But they may thank you for how much you get caught up on in the days leading up to it!

T-Minus 10 Days

Read aloud before getting out of bed in the morning: *"Today, I begin preparing for 5 Fearless Days. This is not a punishment; it's a creative retreat. I choose this because the work I'll produce matters to me, to the people I serve, and to my Uphill Self. My contract is written and signed. Today I take the first small step."*

At any point during the day, complete and check:

- ❑ Turn off all non-essential notifications on your phone leaving only phone calls from key contacts and mission-critical work tools like Slack/Teams/Webex.
- ❑ Complete a 25-minute work block with your phone in another room without context switching or visits to social media pages.
- ❑ After the work block, actively rest by spending 5 sitting in a quiet place with a view or walking alone without headphones.

Reflect: When you tried to focus for 25 minutes, what pulled you away and how did you handle it?

____

____

____

Reflect: What surprised you about today?

____

____

____

T-Minus 9 Days

Read out loud in the morning: *"Today I'm training my brain to finish one thing before starting another. Every distraction I avoid is a rep toward challenge readiness. I build capacity one block at a time."*

Today's checklist:

- ❑ Carry a sticky note or index card and make a mark every time you check your phone.

❑ Complete 2 blocks of 25 minutes each on the same task with 5-minute breaks between (walk, stretch, stairs with no music or podcasts).

How many times did you check your device (no judgment, just data): ___________

Reflect: What triggers do expect to be the loudest during your five-day challenge? What can you do to prepare for them?

____

____

____

____

T-Minus 8 Days

Morning read: *"Environment is more important than willpower. Being smart about what's around me has more impact than discipline. Today I'm designing my workspace and routines with focus as the default."*

Today's checklist:

❑ Complete a 50-minute distraction-free block of work in a quieter, more controlled space than usual - A different room, a library, or closed office. Phone out of the room.

❑ 15-minute rest with no screens or input: Sit quietly, walk, stretch, yoga, etc.

❑ Remove the most tempting and distracting 1 or 2 apps from your phone's home screen, or even better, temporarily delete them.

Reflect: How did this new environment help or hurt your focus?

____

____

What do you need to change about the workspace you
intend to use for your five-day challenge?

____

____

T-Minus 7 Days

Morning read: *"Flow happens when the task is slightly
above my current skill level - Hard enough to engage my
full attention, but not so hard I'm overwhelmed. Today,
I'll find the sweet spot. This is how I build capacity."*

Today's checklist:

- 2 work blocks of 45 minutes each, with a 15-minute
  active silence break between.
- For each block, define the start line (e.g., "Open doc
  and write first paragraph" and finish line (e.g.,
  "Complete rough draft of intro").

Reflect: When did you feel closest to "losing track of time"
today? _______________________________

What conditions were present? (Environment, task type,
energy level, time of day)

____

____

____

____

How can you recreate those conditions on every day of
your challenge?

____

____

T-Minus 6 Days

Morning read: *"When I work, I work hard. When I'm done, I'm done. No half-work, half-scroll. Today I'll discover deep rest is the fuel for deep work. My nervous system needs real recovery to sustain intensity."*

Today's checklist:

- ❑ Morning work block 60 minutes - most important task
- ❑ Later block - 30 minutes on a different but still meaningful task
- ❑ Rule for the day: Monotasking: One browser tab, one document, one task.
- ❑ Offline window: Schedule 2 hours outside your work blocks with no phone, no computer, no checking news or email. Read a book, journal, meditate, exercise or truly rest.

Reflect: What kind of rest actually leaves you feeling more ready to focus later in the day?

What kind of rest makes you feel more drained? (scrolling, TV, etc.)

T-Minus 5 Days

Morning read: *"Boredom, frustration and anxiety are not signs of failure. They are obstacles (rocks & monsters) on the way to flow, which is a daily state for my Uphill Self. Discomfort is more data than danger. Today I'll practice feeling the urge to escape without caving in to it."*

Today's checklist:

- ❑ Two 60-minute work blocks with phone in "airplane mode". Make sure trusted people know you'll be unavailable during these times
- ❑ Two 15-minute active deep rest of your choice

Discomfort protocol: when you feel the urge to check your phone, switch tasks, or escape:

1. **Name the feeling out loud:** "I'm feeling bored/anxious/frustrated"
2. **Breathe**: Take 60 seconds of slow, deep breaths (4-count in, 6-count out)
3. **Recommit:** Say aloud, "I can handle this. I'm sticking with the work"
4. **Resume:** Return to the task without checking devices

Reflect: What feelings made you want to escape to my device or email?

____

____

What happened when you followed the protocol and avoided the escape? (Did the feeling pass? Did you adapt?)

____

____

What did you learn today about your relationship with discomfort?

T-Minus 4 Days: The 3-Hour Challenge

Morning read: *"Today I'll test what's possible when my attention is unfragmented. It's not about perfection. It's an experiment. I'm running a lab to discover how powerful my focus can become when I protect it fiercely. Whatever I learn today will enhance my upcoming five-day challenge."*

Today's checklist:

- ❏ 3 work blocks of 45 minutes each followed by 15-minute breaks
- ❏ Total digital detox: No phone (unless on-call or emergency), no internet, working on an offline computer or on paper.
- ❏ Breaks should be true rest (walk, eat, stretch, no screens)

Reflect: What surprised you about how much you accomplished in 3 hours of truly focused work?

____

____

What friction or resistance did you encounter and how do you plan to deal with it in your pending five-day challenge?

____

____

____

____

T-Minus 3 Days

Morning read: *"I am not someone who 'tries' to focus. I am someone who can sit with the blank page and create value without digital stimulation. Five Fearless Days is not something I'm going to endure - it's about someone I'll become. Today, I'll visualize my Uphill Self standing at the end of those five days."*

Today's checklist:

- [ ] **One 75-90 minute "ultra block"** focused on the work you'll do during your five-day challenge. Outline, draft, download research, set up, make notes, etc.
- [ ] **Define your *5 Fearless Days Challenge* rules** in writing or in your planner:
- [ ] **Device handoff:** Where will your phone be? What is your protocol for true emergencies and how will you be reached?
- [ ] **Allowed tools:** Which devices, apps, software are essential? What's forbidden?
- [ ] **Work hours:** Use the *5 Fearless Days* Planner available for free download at 5fearlessdays.com or a printed calendar or app to schedule your start, stop, rest breaks and mealtimes each day. This structure must be visible to you in advance.
- [ ] **Meals:** What, when, and who prepares. Unless it represents "deep rest" for you, avoid elaborate cooking during your challenge.
- [ ] **Sleep window:** What is your consistent bedtime and wake time?

Visualization: Close your eyes. Imagine it's the final hour of Day 5 of your challenge. You walk up to and merge with your Uphill Self. Look back over the work you've done. How do you feel? What do you see? What do you know about yourself now you didn't know before?

Write 5-10 sentences describing that moment:

____

____

____

____

____

____

____

____

Reflect: What fears come up when you imagine five days without devices?

____

____

What would you like to say to those fears?

____

____

What identity are you climbing into during these coming five days?

____

____

____

T-Minus 2 Days

Morning read: *"My decision to execute 5 Fearless Days is an act of self-leadership, not selfishness. I am doing it with clarity and honesty. Today I set boundaries, clear lose ends and make those who need to know aware of my plan. I'm taking full responsibility for my focus."*

Today's checklist:

- ❏ Complete two blocks of 60 minutes each on work closely related to challenge project
- ❏ Two 15-minute quiet rest breaks
- ❏ Send a message to all who need to know using this template:

"I'm doing a focused five-day work sprints from [Day 1] to [Day 5]. I'll be offline and unreachable except for true emergencies. For urgent matters, contact [backup person]. I'll reconnect on [date]. Thank you for supporting me in this."

Resolve all loose ends: Pay bills, send emails, schedule future appointments, complete grocery shopping.

Reflect: What do you need to forgive or let go of (projects, expectations, perfectionism) to fully commit to Five Fearless Days?

____

____

What would make the challenge feel like a success, even if it doesn't go perfectly?

____

____

T-Minus 1 Day

Morning read: *"Tomorrow is Day One. Today I clarify, rest, and set intention. I have trained. I have prepared. My work environment is in order. It's time to trust the process and honor the work. After today, I am fully ready."*

Today's checklist:

- ❑ One block of no more than 45 minutes early - review, organize, set up files and tools
- ❑ As early as you can, stop all heavy cognitive work for the day
- ❑ Challenge rules for device usage are in effect after lunch. Experience the emotional texture of device separation
- ❑ Finish setting up your 5 Fearless Days Planner or calendar with goals for daily achievement and your schedule
- ❑ Review your contract. If you accomplished a significant portion of your objective during this 10-day training, it may need revision to the upside. That's okay. If you revise it, make sure you re-sign it and show to your AP.
- ❑ Touch base with your AP to set expectations for daily check-in. If they don't hear from you, you must hear from them.
- ❑ Bedtime should be unhurried and at the same time as your scheduled time for challenge days.

Reflect: How do you feel as you lay down to sleep on the eve of your 5 Fearless Days?

____

____

____

What do you hope for? What do you fear?

____

____

____

What do you need to remember if things get hard?

____

____

What do you think your Uphill Self would tell you speaking from the perspective of the end of Day Five?

____

____

____

____

____

____

Procrastination Versus Preparation

If you skimmed through the 10-day program and thought, "this is pretty much my life as it already is", you're in a good place. You'll require minimal preparation to reach full readiness for your challenge.

Others, however, will be closer to panic mode: *"Are you kidding me, Mike? Three hours of creative work on one day? I don't have time for it. Have you seen my life, my responsibilities? I have kids! My job is driving a forklift in a warehouse. That's why I'm considering this challenge in the first place. I need to take PTO from work and get a sitter!"*

Take it easy, you're still on track. This is just a sign ten days may not be enough to get you in position for a successful challenge. You'll need a more extensive run-up like the 30-day program found in the appendix. Make no mistake, the effort will be worth it, and your Uphill Self will thank you later. But you can't go "cold turkey" from a non-stop, physically demanding carnival of a life filled with intermittent escape-scrolling into five days of "sitting in the silence" and building something meaningful. Your brain won't be ready, and your body will want to sleep and binge through the whole thing.

So determine the amount of time you need, and follow a program similar to either the one above or the one in the appendix, depending on the number of day you have.

Planning the Schedule for Your 5 Fearless Days

On the eve of Day One, set all of your proverbial ducks in a row.

Your workspace should be a room you control access to and one in which you have high odds of remaining undisturbed. Tools should be charged up, lined up and ready to go. The last thing you want on Day One is the distraction of a sudden need to go shopping or await a delivery. Expectations should be set with housemates and loved ones. At work, all they need to know is that you're on vacation. Design the perfect answer to *"Going anyplace fun?"*

Your emergency protocol should be in place. If you can, prepare to work like it's 1987, with the landline disconnected from the jack. Of course, there could be exceptions. If you're a doctor on call, you'll need to have very specific notifications enabled. If you're a parent of minors, they'll need access to you. Use your discretion, but for heaven's sake don't have a live phone sitting on your desk all day.

During your training and preparation, if not before, you've become aware of what your best "pomodoro" cadence is: Do you prefer the "standard" 25-minute work blocks paired with 5-minute breaks, the longer 45/15 "flow" blocks, or the intense "ultra" 90/15 work marathons? Some people prefer to use all three at different times of the day. Others like to stick with the same rhythm throughout. There is no "best" method for everyone.

Tools designed specifically for scheduling five-day challenges are available for free at 5fearlessdays.com, including a useful online planner that will take your preferences for start, end, meals, and work/break cadences. This app will generate your schedule and gamify your accomplishment to make it fun. If you prefer to keep your schedule offline, you'll find a printable PDF serving the same purpose.

It's strongly suggested your schedule be identical for each of the five days to maintain rhythm and routine.

The next chapter should be read immediately after this one for the first time, and again when you wake up on the morning of Day One of 5 Fearless Days. But first: Double-checking you've completed the items below is essential to what comes next.

ACTIONS TO COMPLETE BEFORE MOVING ON:

- ❑ Look at your calendar to determine how many days between now and Day One of your challenge. It should be at least ten days out.
- ❑ Review the ten-day training program in this chapter and make sure you're prepared to follow it starting at T-minus ten days.
- ❑ If you have 30 days or more before your challenge, review the longer training program in the Appendix of this book.
- ❑ Prepare the schedule for your 5 Fearless Days challenge using tools available at 5fearlessdays.com or those of your choice.

In The Arena

This chapter contains separate sections for each of your *5 Fearless Days*. It's intended to be read at least twice and kept bookmarked for use during your challenge.

1. Read it now
2. Read it the evening before Day One
3. Read the section for **each day** the evening before

Take a deep breath.

With the inhalation of oxygen and the other elements of air, mix in some gratitude. What you have in front of you, five days set apart as sacred space on the X-axis of your life, is rare and precious. For much of human history and in many places around the world, the privilege of using time for this purpose was unthinkable for the great majority.

Read this quote with care:

> "It is not the critic who counts; not the man who points out how the strong man stumbles, or where the doer of deeds could have done them better. The credit belongs to the man who is actually in the arena, whose face is marred by dust and sweat and blood; who strives valiantly; who errs, who comes short again and again, because there is no effort without error and shortcoming; but who does actually strive to do the deeds; who knows great enthusiasms, the great devotions; who spends himself in a worthy cause; who at the best knows in the end the triumph of high achievement, and who at the worst, if he fails, at least fails while daring greatly, so that his place shall never be with those cold and timid souls who neither know victory nor defeat."
>
> -- Theodore Roosevelt

As someone who has committed to an epic five-day challenge in pursuit of something meaningful and significant, you're in a unique position. Whoever you are, whatever your objective, you are now the "doer of deeds", the "man (or woman) who is actually in the arena".

Every "arena", and every *5 Fearless Days* challenge, is as unique and individual as the person under contract to complete it.

My experience includes several of my own five-day challenges, augmented by my work with many more individuals and their unique and specific objectives. Still, I can only guess at the feelings you'll face during your first one and provide general advice for each day. Your initial experience may be smooth and satisfying, or it may feel like being pressed into a cheese grater. Your first-time experience depends on many factors including your readiness, habits, abilities, beliefs and attitudes.

This chapter is not meant to serve as an hour-by-hour planner or tracker for your challenge. Tools for that purpose, ranging from a printable PDF for working offline to a web app powered by AI are available for free at 5fearlessdays.com.

As you read through the section for each day, visualize yourself at the point where you first encounter some feeling of resistance. These words are meant to linger in your mind as a secondary Accountability Partner as you go to sleep before each day dawns.

5 Fearless Days

Day One: Persist

What are you addicted to?

What do you *want* to be addicted to?

Take these two questions to bed with you the night before Day One.

Your addictions likely became obvious and visible during your training program. They're the things you badly wanted to do instead when you sat down to complete your work blocks.

But what if?

What if those same itchy cravings for things like scrolling, snacking and loafing could be transferred to an overwhelming desire to do creative work every day?

You know author J.K. Rowling as the creator of the *Harry Potter* universe, a vast work of the imagination she began writing longhand as a single mother on welfare in the mid-1990s. What fewer people know is *since* becoming a billionaire from the proceeds of *Harry Potter*, she has gone on to write 9 novels for adults, including a complex 8-volume detective series written under a pseudonym totaling over 6,000 pages.

Imagine for a moment the options a person with a billion dollars has each morning. Then imagine them choosing to sit down and hammer out two million more words in black and white. What do you think J.K. Rowling is addicted to?

You will become addicted to whatever you anticipate most.

For some, it's the burn of whiskey sliding down their throat at the end of a hard day, signaling a blood-alcohol level rising to escape velocity. Just one of many dead-ends of selfishness serving no one and accomplish nothing.

Pornography, candy, cocaine, flick-and-gawk doom scrolling - there's little difference in what any of these substances do to your brain, and treating any of them as "harmless" is a staggering display of ignorance and naivete.

Whatever your relationship with purposeless addictions, you're *under contract* to set them aside for these five days to re-wire into something else entirely. A major objective of this challenge is to allow your attention to be fully captured by your work. **You seek to be hooked.**

"But Mike, I don't wanna become a workaholic."

Stop right there, because that word is a Tomorrowist diversion. It's often weaponized by people who prefer you join them in *their* addictions. Misery loves company. By equating your newfound joy in creative work with alcohol dependency and neglect of other responsibilities, they shame you back to the status quo *they* want you to persist in.

Don't fall for it. Don't listen to or use a word that doesn't and won't apply to you.

As the sun rises on Day One, you are delivering on a commitment you made to fulfill a singular purpose with hours you have set aside. You have made intentional arrangements to remain reasonably undisturbed during this time. Barring emergency, you will follow through. This is not any kind of *-ism*. This is integrity.

We're all "addictive personalities". It's not like you can purge dopamine from your system. It's always there. But you choose your dealer. Is it the shady character in a hoodie down on the corner? The smiling barista at Starbucks? The social media mogul cruising the seven seas in his 300-foot yacht?

Not today. Today the only dealer is the vision you want brought into reality. The job no one else on earth can do. It's the only source you're buying dope from today.

The problem? You may not be fully wired into it yet. You feel the pull of your phone calling from the other room. The itch for *anything else*. Maybe the page is too blank. You need a drink. A snack. Suddenly the clock seems to drag and time is stretched. Prepare to face a feeling you've been conditioned to call "boredom", but in reality is a high-density existence you will come to crave.

Just persist.

Comedian Jerry Seinfeld, also a billionaire and over seventy years old with no obligation to do anything "hard" ever again, shuts himself in a windowless room with nothing but a chair, a legal pad and pen. He doesn't have to write jokes, but he doesn't allow himself to do anything else. He's a long-term addict to the hard work of mining humor from everyday life, and the anticipated laughter of large crowds in response to its practiced delivery. The result? Continuously sold-out residencies in Las Vegas and New York City performing the material from that windowless room. What do you think Jerry Seinfeld is addicted to? He *persists*.

Beyond the roughly 20% of your contracted work getting done, this is your simple assignment for Day One: Persist. Even if it feels like moving through a thicket of thorns at times. You're not used to this. Would you like to be?

Getting addicted to your work won't go down like eating "just one" Oreo or potato chip. Hard work is not crack. It's not carbolicious. It's high-protein, high-fiber and packed with bitter vitamins. One day it will be a long-and-slow burning source of renewable energy, but today it feels like trying to start a fire by rubbing two sticks together.

Your work, if aligned to a strong purpose, will eventually become addictive. Just two very prominent examples from a long list of many, many successful creators are cited above. The hook *will* be set if you persist. If you followed your training program, the change of dopamine dealers has already begun.

Starting today, you lock it in.

Persist.

THE EVENING BEFORE DAY ONE:

- ❏ Tour your workspace one last time and make sure everything is ready, including your hourly schedule.
- ❏ Touch base with your AP via text or phone. Share both your excitement and any feelings of apprehension for the coming day.
- ❏ Review your signed contract. Are you ready to deliver another 20%? Focus on quantity. Quality comes later. The Perfectionist and the Tomorrowist within you are the same person. They have not paid the price of admission and do not belong in the arena with you.
- ❏ Just before drifting off to sleep, visualize yourself "entering the arena" armed with everything you need for a successful, victorious creative day.
- ❏ Strictly adhere to your challenge bedtime and set your alarm for your challenge wake time whether you need it or not!

Day Two: Face the Beast

Day One is in the books.

If you're like most challengers, you learned much about yourself. Your limits. Your potential. Maybe you surprised yourself, impressed with the quantity and quality of your output. Maybe you're a little disappointed in what ultimately came out of you. Maybe it's part of your nature: You tend to doubt yourself and even expect disappointment.

Either way, it's only one day.

Day Two is brand new. It's also only one day. So don't bother to think about the "sophomore slump" or the "second album inferior to the first" because you don't have enough data to even review at this point.

You're likely to face a new enemy on Day Two.

Distraction is simple enough to deal with in mechanical ways. Simply remove it. Be in a place where it is not, and do not allow it to enter where you are. It is external, and you keep it that way.

But what of the Resistance arising from within?

What of the "powers that be" established deep within your subconscious mind - the root causes behind why you have not already done what you are setting out to do? The voices of "no", and "not enough", and "not yet", and "something's just not right."

Do you think they'll stand idly by while you tip-toe past with your plan and your precious little contract? Think they'll stay mute when you sit down and try to do something with an intensity and for a duration you've never done before?

It's not about making liars of them. They've always been liars.

Their very survival is on the line.

I'm talking about them as if they're alive, as if they're a part of you.

When you use the phrase "every fiber of my being", this is what you're talking about. These beliefs, these contradictions, these *antagonists* are woven into your very fibers and tissues.

They are not you, but you host them like you might wind up hosting a tapeworm if you consumed an under-cooked pork chop.

Sorry, that's gross.

But it's important to recognize the parasitical nature of these beliefs.

It's crucial to understand, they thrive in a homeostatic environment, where conditions are always the same. They will fight to preserve those conditions. Abrupt changes are dangerous to them, and sustained change is deadly.

A dead parasite is systematically broken down by the host's immune system and removed as waste.

You have long-time freeloaders aboard whose time has come. But their survival instincts, which you can easily mistake for your own, will kick in with this challenge and put up a final boss fight.

This is what we refer to as Resistance.

Notice I use a capital "R". This is an homage to Steven Pressfield's remarkable little book *The War of Art*. Re-reading this book periodically has been like a booster vaccination against my own Resistance, preventing the parasites from establishing new infections.

Pressfield doesn't use the parasite metaphor – that's my own conceit. He describes Resistance as a universal force affecting everyone from artists to entrepreneurs. It manifests as procrastination, fear, self-criticism, overthinking, busyness and all other forms of self-sabotage.

The solution he suggests in *The War of Art* is to recognize Resistance as an external enemy, not an internal failing, and to *push through it* to do the work that matters.

A parasite is an external or foreign body thriving on energy and resources not belonging to it. When you, the host, withhold those resources and create a hostile environment, it must leave or die. Viruses thrive in cells at body temperatures near normal. The body's defense mechanism of raising its temperature several degrees prevents their replication and often wipes them out in a matter of hours.

Your five-day challenge incites a deliberate fever. Work "feverishly" on Day Two and simply ignore thoughts, voices and impulses not serving your purpose. Let them burn themselves out.

There is no permanent immunity. There may come a day when the forces of Resistance return in full force. A day on which you cave in and allow yourself to be dragged back to the homeostatic baseline you were at before. A day looking too much like last year.

But as Aragorn said at the Black Gate in his famous "Sons of Gondor" speech in the movie *The Return of the King*, "It is not this day."

Day Two is not that day. Today you will face the Beast Resistance, and today you will win.

THE EVENING BEFORE DAY TWO:

- ❑ Complete a journal entry - a few sentences describing what you did on Day One and the feelings you experienced, both positive and distracting.
- ❑ Touch base with your AP via text or phone or simply share your journal entry. Don't hold back. Take their response to sleep with you, looking forward to the coming day.
- ❑ Review your signed contract. Are you ready to deliver another 20%? Focus on quantity. Quality comes later.

Day Three: Keep Yourself Honest

Much has been written about the importance of a positive mindset in any form of accomplishment. Human psychology is a deep and well-researched science, a rabbit-hole we could all wander down for more hours than any of us have left in a useful lifespan. Unless it's your life's work, it should remain incidental to what IS your life's work.

The study of making yourself do something becomes moot if nothing gets done.

You'll wake up tomorrow to Day Three of challenge mode. We don't have time to do a full rehab on your mindset. We need to get something DONE first. Proof will take you further than anything you can glean from content. You already have two days of output to look at. Look at and admire the quantity. Ignore the quality for now.

Be careful how you talk to yourself as you review your work.

If a set of verbal affirmations spoken aloud as you look in the mirror is part of your morning routine, don't stop now - but think about changing them up.

If you're still scared and procrastinating after months or years of repeating affirmations, and you don't seem to have "reprogrammed" your mind, *5 Fearless Days* should serve as a major element in the solution.

A spoken affirmation statement is heard by your subconscious mind and evaluated in a binary way: TRUE or FALSE.

Let's say you stand in front of the mirror and shout *"I have ten million dollars and a Lamborghini"* ten times before brushing your teeth. Meanwhile your subconscious mind is well aware your savings account balance is $127.33 and the car in your uncovered parking space is a 1997 Toyota Corolla with a front bumper secured by duct tape.

Speaking something **potentially** true is unconvincing to a subconscious mind with a B.S. meter on high alert.

On the other hand, as a software developer you could shout "I'm a master coder and write at least 200 lines of functional code every day!" If you actually *did* write 200 lines of functional code yesterday and have time and intention set aside to do it again today, and tomorrow, and the day after, truth is detected and reinforced. "Master coder" doesn't sound dreamy and ridiculous; it sounds **increasingly** *true.*

Continue to match the truth of what you say with the truth of what you do on a daily basis with enough consistency and reliability *tested by adversity*, and what you state will become **inevitably** true. That's a power with a sacred precedent we'll revisit here:

"In the beginning, God created..."

There we have it, within the first five words of scripture. The Creator asserts his identity as a creative. When he says "Let there be light", is anyone surprised when light appears, followed by everything else in the order specified by the Creator? You are created in the image of the founding creative being. Clearly we humans, flawed as we are, are creators, because look at what's here that wasn't here before us. And yet, if you hear a hundred people say "I wanna write a book," how many books from those hundred actually wind up on shelves?

This isn't esoteric New Age magic. It's simple honesty.

Calling someone a liar is universally hypocritical, because we all lie to some extent. Some lies get called out, the teller of tales exposed on the evening news. Others remain hidden in darkness until everyone involved is dead and buried. We like to minimize lies that "don't hurt others", but there is no such thing. Every untruth has real consequences to real people.

You have a Contract with yourself for these five days. If your obligation is 150 pages of draft, the only way to "keep yourself honest" is to produce 150+ pages of draft. Sleeping at the end of Day Five with 77, 138 or even 149 pages is an epic fail that could haunt you for as long as it takes you to reverse and disprove it. Without any valid mitigating circumstance (like an unavoidable emergency making your objective physically impossible), the message you're sending deep into your subconscious is *"I don't have what it takes. I say one thing and do less. I quit within sight of the finish line."*

Not going to happen on Day Three.

The middle of a five-day work week is often called "Hump Day". On Day Three you'll reach the halfway point. At lunchtime you should have around 50% of your outlined challenge work done. It doesn't have to be exact, but should be close.

You're in a place on the timeline with multiple days behind you and multiple days ahead. You have a double dose of what it means to use the most valuable asset in your life, time, in a better way than you have in the past. The past has passed, and as good as the last two days have been, don't get caught up in the rosy cinematic picture of your future. Pay no attention to the part of you still preaching the false tenets of Tomorrowism. The next day is outside your current scope of control. Right now, you are committed to the fervent and devout practice of radical Todayism. Your next "today" is Day Three.

A fine day to keep yourself honest.

THE EVENING BEFORE DAY THREE:

- ❏ Complete a journal entry - a few sentences describing what you did on Day Two and the feelings you experienced, both positive and distracting.
- ❏ Touch base with your AP via text or phone or simply share your journal entry. Don't hold back. Take their response to sleep with you, looking forward to the coming day.
- ❏ Review your signed contract. Are you ready to deliver another 20%? Focus on quantity. Quality comes later. Just get it done.

Day Four: Never, Ever Quit

No matter how well you've prepared and how "psyched up" you are for your challenge, odds are high at some point during these five days you'll experience a quit impulse.

I may be wrong. I've worked with a couple of people who moved through their challenges like a heated knife through butter. I've even experienced a near-flawless challenge of my own, where I got more out of each hour and day than I expected.

For most creators, there's still some of what Rocky Balboa calls "stuff in the basement" needing to shoulder past some hairy, muscular obstacles in order to ascend the stairs into the light of day.

These often manifest as thoughts like:

This really sucks. I should just shred it all and start over. (first draft angst)

I'm really not very good at this. My work doesn't even resemble what (insert name of advanced role model) does. (comparison)

This was a bad idea. I could be on the beach right now! (FOMO)

I'm really tired. Maybe this is enough. I'll get a fresh start with my morning caffeine (Tomorrowism)

These thoughts tend to stack, leading to amplification of their destructive potential:

I got a lot done today already! I know I committed to five hours, but what I have after 3.5 hours is worth celebrating. Also, I'm hungry. Also, my friends are going to see a new movie tonight without me! I'll do double tomorrow and I feel good about it! (completion bias teaming up with FOMO to preach orthodox Tomorrowism).

Let's pause right here and acknowledge: We've got issues. If we allow it, we will talk ourselves out of fulfilling our contract. We'll revert to default behaviors leading to where we were before: Stuck as Chuck in pickup truck.

Your first five-day challenge is not the time to psycho-analyze yourself and create a game plan for mental spring cleaning. Over-consumption of self-help is a factor in getting you where you are, and we're putting everything aside except for two blunt instruments:

1. Abrupt state changes
2. Relentless professionalism

The first is simple in execution. When you recognize an undesirable thought pattern (anything suggesting you stop short of your contractual terms for the day), you move swiftly to interrupt it.

Example: It's an hour after lunch and you have 700 words left to go for the day. Your fingers hover over the keyboard as you consider the intricate phrasing for a sentence you want to get just right. Suddenly, you hear that voice and start feeling those feels:

"Maybe you should just--"

"This might be a good place to--"

"Sleeping on this tough spot might be--"

This where you make those mental em-dashes, stand up quickly and say out loud with conviction, "No! Not having this. Eat my dust, Resistance!" followed by ten jumping jacks, push-ups or squats. Then sit down, crack your knuckles, mutter "Stand back. Outta the way. I'm coming for you," and resume from the location of your blinking cursor.

Sound extreme? Afraid family and neighbors will think you've finally lost it, or maybe you've developed Tourette's syndrome?

I followed this exact protocol during a five-day challenge where I ended with 37,901 words of a fantasy novel draft (151 pages). This output exceeded my deliberately stretched objective for the challenge by 2,901 words.

I also did a lot of calisthenics not specified in my original Contract.

My big takeaway from that challenge is what I perceived as a block or fatigue was almost always a **lack of sufficient blood flow** getting to the deeper neurons required to continue.

Creativity is certainly a *spiritual* thing. It's also very *physiological*. No human work is manifested in the physical world without interaction of mind, body and material.

Creative activities like writing, coding, drawing, painting or crocheting are ostensibly sedentary, usually done seated or standing and fixed in one location for hours at a time.

Brief, intense physical movement can act as both cleansing refresh and catalyst. By exerting your body and forcing your muscles to demand an increased intake of oxygen-rich air into your lungs, through the pump of your heart and ultimately into your bloodstream, you move the molecules making creativity happen.

Everyone's built different. I found a real sweet-spot in the "pomodoro" technique of working for 25 minutes followed by a break including a minute of exercise and conscious state-changing speech. The break between each session is scheduled to be five minutes, but I find myself chomping at the bit to get back to writing after 2-4 minutes of jumping or walking around saying strong words out loud.

Others I've talked to would be annoyed out of their mind to be interrupted after 25 minutes, especially if they're deep into the flow of their work. They extend their poms to an hour or even 90 minutes. Some ignore the clock completely and break only when their brain naturally comes out of the creative trance.

In any case, chaining yourself to your desk for 8 to 10 hours without a break as a form of discipline is not a good idea. Acknowledge the physiological nature of your creativity and feed it the fuel it needs, which includes air and flowing blood.

Be a Professional

One of Steven Pressfield's follow-up books to *The War of Art* is the equally valuable *Turning Pro*. In this work, he defines a professional as someone who is committed to their craft above all else, regardless of inspiration, mood, or external rewards.

Many of us carry a connotation of professionalism causing us to wrinkle our noses in disgust. After all, it's the corporate work-a-day world we're trying to escape from. The last thing we want to hear is about how our success in our most personal and intimate creative endeavors is dependent on clocking in and out on time every day.

"I like to do my creative work on my own time, when I most feel like it. Sometimes I'm just really into it. Other times I'm not. I gotta go with the flow, man."

I hope you can see where I'm going with this. *Five Fearless Days* is rooted in the reader's desire to catalyze the completion of something magnificent, and set the stage for more to come. Much more. It's not meant for the hobbyist or fair-weather dabbler who just wants to "try something" or "see if this is for me."

I'm assuming my readers are either professional in their attitude toward their work or aspire to be so.

To check the barometer of your own status as a professional, here are some key aspects Pressfield points out in his work:

- **Showing up every day:** The professional establishes a routine and adheres to it consistently, treating their creative endeavor like a job.

- **Committing to the long haul:** They are patient and dedicated over the long term, understanding that mastery requires sustained effort and not immediate gratification.

- **Acting in the face of fear:** The professional acknowledges fear but does not wait for it to disappear before starting or continuing their work.

- **Accepting no excuses:** Only a few valid reasons (like a health crisis) are acceptable for missing work; all other forms of self-sabotage are dismissed.

- **Mastering technique:** They dedicate themselves to learning and refining their craft, and are not afraid to ask for help or seek instruction.

- **Seeking order:** The professional eliminates chaos and distraction from their environment to create a space conducive to work.

- **Not taking failure or success personally:** The professional focuses on the work itself and does not let external praise or criticism dictate their self-worth or affect their routine.

- **Self-validating:** They judge their progress by their own internal standards and whether they have been true to their calling, rather than relying on the opinions of others.

Do those points make you feel like shredding your Contract and stuffing your creative work squarely into the realm of "side-hustle"?

Or did you find yourself nodding along to those bullet points muttering. *"Yep. That's me. Let's roll."*?

Maybe you're still putting food on the table from the proceeds of your 9 to 5. I'm not asking you to flip the bird in the general direction of your benevolent employer and go all-in on something that has yet to pay you a dollar.

Keep the lights on, but maintain your professional attitude as you transition from one role to another – every day. You remain employed because you show up and generally meet the expectations documented in your job description. These are aspects of professionalism and include adhering to certain common-sense rules and etiquette going beyond HR policy and regulations.

The difference between the hours you've sold off (contracted) to someone else and the hours committed to your creative work is important. When the clock switches over to YOU time, you become an entrepreneur, like it or not. Maybe you haven't thought about yourself in that way. Maybe you have no interest in marketing or selling anything, making payroll or doing "business stuff".

That's okay. There's nothing worse than watching months peel off the calendar, then years, as you meticulously support someone else's goals and objectives when you have your own. Often this work is for an organization so large you're not sure what the objective is. In return you get to pay the rent, eat food, and flush indoor toilets. Most people are quite content with this trade-off, and to take whatever's left after the bills are paid to entertain themselves on weekends and after hours.

But not you. You build, write, sculpt, paint, code or assemble something your own. You're tempted when your friends invite you to join them in "winding down", and there's nothing wrong with consciously scheduled recreation, but "spare time" is not something needing to be killed. Not to you.

As you go into Day Four:

Choose to be a professional.

Disrupt thoughts that drag you down.

Move as a means to keep your work moving.

THE EVENING BEFORE DAY FOUR:

- ❑ Complete a journal entry - a few sentences describing what you did on Day Three and the feelings you experienced, both positive and distracting.
- ❑ Touch base with your AP via text or phone or simply share your journal entry. Don't hold back. Take their response to sleep with you, looking forward to the coming day.
- ❑ Review your signed contract. Are you ready to deliver another 20%? Focus on quantity. Quality comes later. Just get it done.
- ❑ Think about how you respond to thoughts suggesting you quit early or defer work to the following day. How will you disrupt these and get back to the work?
- ❑ Consider what you do during your breaks. What do you do away from your workspace to insulate yourself from distraction and reset yourself for another session? Is there enough physical movement in your breaks?
- ❑ Review the aspects of a Professional and how they apply to you. Are you committed to a professional lifestyle or are you a hobbyist or "weekender"?

Day Five: Finish Strong

Obedience.

Does the word spike any discomfort? If your parents demanded unquestioned *obedience* from the young you with strict physical or emotional consequences for failure, you're feeling a bit of residual pain now.

Maybe you have a child or friend who acts or has acted in what you consider a *disobedient* way, putting themselves and others in danger or squandering what you see as their potential with their unwise decisions.

Obedience also describes our willingness to keep the rules and commandments of gods and governments. These laws make sense to most people most of the time, and carry serious consequences (Thou shalt not kill), while others have become somewhat open to interpretation (SPEED LIMIT 65 MPH, Thou shalt not commit adultery).

What does *obedience* mean in the context of your five-day challenge?

It's the eve of Day Five, the day on which you'll either proclaim *finished* or *failure*.

You should be around 80% done with your work at this point, but every challenge is different. I've seen people who have already exceeded their goal by the end of Day Four. I've seen others who weren't yet at the halfway point. Some had lost interest and quit. Others finally overcame their procrastination and leveraged the deadline to finish more than half of their work on Day Five alone!

Is "get back to work" an order you can give yourself with confidence it'll be obeyed?

There is no boss present. No distant corporate entity to submit reports to. No annual performance review.

There's just you and your AP. Someone who, if chosen properly, will remind you of and amplify your decision and commitment. But your AP will not always know when you're struggling. Will you reach out at these times with a call or text message, or would you "rather not bother" your AP?

This is why YOU are the agent. The only one you need to obey. Sure, once you get a great AP on the line, you'll get an earful. *"So, you're thinking of quitting with just 146 lines of new code because you're "tired"? Come on, you're better than that. Get on it, and call me when you're done. I'll be waiting."*

This conversation is unlikely to happen unless you are self-directed enough to reach out at the right time. Unless you are obedient to your own self-directive.

The consequences of disobedience to your contract won't kill you or make you a bad person. They're just heartbreaking. There are no jack-booted enforcers coming to arrest you. No fines will be assessed. Your AP should levy some social consequences, which may max out with an eye roll and disappointed shake of the head.

Does that matter to you? Are you motivated to avoid your AP's disappointment or disgust?

If you carry a preconceived reputation as a serial quitter from your past experience, the only way out of the gravitational pull of your comfort zone is discomfort – reaching escape velocity through massive five-day action.

You've been in the arena for four days, and only one remains to endure and enjoy. Look at the distance between you and your goal and measure yourself for the podium.

There's only one boss, and you're wearing the uniform.

Obey or die.

Not literally. But if you know, you know.

THE EVENING BEFORE DAY FIVE:

- ❑ Complete a journal entry - a few sentences describing what you did on Day Four and the feelings you experienced, both positive and distracting.
- ❑ Review your signed contract one last time. Are you ready to deliver the final 20%? Focus on quantity. Quality comes later. Just get it done.
- ❑ Touch base with your AP via text or phone or simply share your journal entry. Don't hold back. Take their response to sleep with you, looking forward to the coming day.
- ❑ Think about how you respond to thoughts suggesting you quit early or defer work to the following day. How will you disrupt these and get back to the work?
- ❑ Reconsider the meaning of the word obedience in your mind and ask yourself if you are willing to obey your own self-direction.

How Did it Go?

Read this section after you've completed Day Five.

Of course I hope you're celebrating. Basking in a mighty sense of completion. If you're using the gamified online planner, a banner with five beautiful trophies lined up appeared when you earn 95% or more of the possible challenge points.

Success means you have a body of work that felt beyond your ability just five days ago.

Failure means you let yourself down, *this time*, but you're still alive and you're a good person. You'll be back.

In either case, what you learned about yourself needs to be captured, or the details and insights gained will vanish like dreams do after you wake up and start another day.

As the creator of this *5 Fearless Days* protocol, I'm immensely curious.

It serves you and me both if you take a few minutes to write to me about your experience using the Contact Form on 5fearlessdays.com. Tell me all about it, the good and the bad. Let me know how this book could have been a better guide for you during this process. If you're comfortable with it, share one or more of your daily journal entries with me. Your feedback will enable more effective future editions of this book.

What's Next?

There are two huge risks present at the end of Day Five, risks amplified on the morning of Day Six, the first post-challenge day. Unless you take immediate action against these risks, the result of your first challenge, no matter how impressive they are to you now, will soon be degraded from today's artifact to tomorrow's relic, next month's footnote, and next year's fossil.

Don't let it happen.

The two risks are:

1. You'll sit on what you created during your challenge for too long, and when you finally circle back to it, it looks like crap and you set it aside to move on to the next shiny thing.

2. You'll lose all creative momentum by jumping back into "real life" and getting "caught up", which in short order returns you to homeostasis in the same way your home's thermostat brings the temperature back to 70 degrees. Bottom line? The exact same life you had before you prepared for this challenge.

Clearly you don't want so succumb to either or both of those risks. So what's your insurance against them?

Read the next two chapters of this book, which also happen to be the last two chapters, and follow the instructions found in them.

ACTIONS TO COMPLETE BEFORE MOVING ON:

- ❑ Upon completion of a successful challenge: Teach yourself the lesson that hard work results in pleasant and comfortable rewards. Award yourself something you've held back as delayed gratification.
- ❑ Coming off of an unsuccessful challenge: Beating yourself up is pointless. You simply need to try again. Review your contract, your planner, and your journal entries. Where do you think you went wrong and when? Was it an insufficient training time-frame? Do you have underlying beliefs still unaddressed? What will you do differently next time? Plan for the *next time* starting today.
- ❑ Say this out loud: *"This is only the beginning. With this first challenge I have accessed only the tiniest fraction of my potential. I won't lose momentum and I'll never stop."*
- ❑ Read Chapters Seven and Eight of this book as soon as possible.

Good and Faithful

Applying Ancient Wisdom to Your Continuation

This chapter is meant to be read in the 24-48 hours immediately following the completion of a *5 Fearless Days* challenge, when the two risks described at the end of the last chapter are at their highest. Read this during the hiatus, the sabbatical between an intense challenge and the "bridge" of a more normal routine between challenges.

Your five days are finished. The challenge is done. The result was binary - you either fulfilled your contract or you didn't. If you didn't, you failed. But no failure is permanent and every person we label "successful" failed many times. Today is a day of rest from your creative work, which needs to sit and marinate before being improved and polished.

Let's look at a story told two thousand years ago by Jesus and recorded by his disciple Matthew, a former tax collector for the Roman occupiers.

Now, before you decide this chapter is not for you because you don't believe in the Bible and don't want to be preached at, consider: This story was told to a group of people who had never heard the word "Christian" and weren't sitting in Sunday School.

The story was originally told in or around Jerusalem during the week of Passover, when the city was crowded with international visitors. It was told by a man who within five days or so would be condemned for blasphemy by the religious leaders of his own people and nailed to a wooden cross.

The teachings of Jesus of Nazareth have not survived for two millennia for nothing. Their depth and meaning stand as the primary evidence, as conveyed by the recorded writings of several witnesses, that this stuff wasn't just "made up". These teachings are powerful artifacts.

Jesus used brief stories, or parables, like the one we're about to consider to make points at several levels. There was the casual audience, those who followed him out of curiosity to see if maybe they could catch a glimpse of one of those cool miracles they'd heard about. There were the truth seekers, those hoping to glean something life-changing from his words. Finally, there was the inner circle, those who ate, drank and walked with him every day.

We'll apply this parable at our own level, which is of creative people still somewhat unsure of our own potential but strongly wanting to make the most of it. We're not doing this just to "make money", although creative production is certainly worthy of financial compensation equal to its value. We're doing it because it's good and right, and because NOT doing it feels bad and wrong.

Am I "twisting scripture" by using the parable in this way? I think not. If you believe in God or any supreme force, you'll also believe in the purpose behind your talent. What's the point of natural abilities if not to bring them to full fruition with the time, space and energy allotted to you?

Jesus himself expressed his own creativity through storytelling, ostensibly tying his mini-tales back to "the kingdom of heaven" while setting them in the hardscrabble world for our understanding.

Without further explanation or justification, I will produce the entirety of this brief story below from the New International Version (NIV), which is currently the best-selling English translation.

THE PARABLE OF THE BAGS OF GOLD

"Again, it will be like a man going on a journey, who called his servants and entrusted his wealth to them. To one he gave five bags of gold, to another two bags, and to another one bag, each according to his ability. Then he went on his journey. The man who had received five bags of gold went at once and put his money to work and gained five bags more. So also, the one with two bags of gold gained two more. But the man who had received one bag went off, dug a hole in the ground and hid his master's money.

After a long time the master of those servants returned and settled accounts with them. The man who had received five bags of gold brought the other five. 'Master,' he said, 'you entrusted me with five bags of gold. See, I have gained five more.'

His master replied, 'Well done, good and faithful servant! You have been faithful with a few things; I will put you in charge of many things. Come and share your master's happiness!'

The man with two bags of gold also came. 'Master,' he said, 'you entrusted me with two bags of gold; see, I have gained two more.'

His master replied, 'Well done, good and faithful servant! You have been faithful with a few things; I will put you in charge of many things. Come and share your master's happiness!'

Then the man who had received one bag of gold came. 'Master,' he said, 'I knew that you are a hard man, harvesting where you have not sown and gathering where you have not scattered seed. So I was afraid and went out and hid your gold in the ground. See, here is what belongs to you.'

His master replied, 'You wicked, lazy servant! So you knew that I harvest where I have not sown and gather where I have not scattered seed? Well then, you should have put my money on deposit with the bankers, so that when I returned I would have received it back with interest.

'So take the bag of gold from him and give it to the one who has ten bags. For whoever has will be given more, and they will have an abundance. Whoever does not have, even what they have will be taken from them. And throw that worthless servant outside, into the darkness, where there will be weeping and gnashing of teeth.' "

A Fearless Interpretation

The King James Version of the Bible names this story "The Parable of the Talents", from the Greek word *talanton*, a measure of weight somewhere close to 75 pounds. For reference, 75 pounds of pure gold as of this writing has a market value of just over six million US dollars. It was certainly a huge fortune in biblical times.

Talanton is the root from which our modern-day word *talent* derives, referring to innate human abilities and facilities.

Things we are *given*. Gifts.

Whether you think of them as God-given, distributed by the universe, genetic lottery wins or glitches in the matrix, you have to admit these things are cosmic handouts you apparently did nothing to earn or deserve in their initial, embryonic form.

In the story, the "master" distributes these enormous sums of wealth to three unnamed "servants". We'll call them One, Two, and Three. They each receive different sums "according to his ability".

This is the first critical point: God, the Universe, or Whatever does not hand out these wonderful abilities to people who don't have the wherewithal to develop them. ***If you have it, you can max it out, otherwise you wouldn't have it. Acknowledging this truth is the key to unlocking your potential.***

Michael Jordan and Kobe Bryant were born as certified five-baggers who not only recognized the size of their basketball talent allocation, they also discerned the level of effort it would take to double it and retire as ten-baggers.

Notice these distributions of wealth come with no specific instructions from the Master regarding their handling. No *"I need this doubled by the time I get back"* or even *"do your best"*. All three servants are left to figure out on their own both what to do with the money and what the expected results were to be. All they had to go on was their knowledge of the character of their master and their previous experience. We are told specifically that those gifted with more had shown more "ability" in the past, prompting a larger starting allocation.

The master's message was, in essence, *"Here you go. I trust each of you based on what I've seen from you. I'm outta here, but I'll be back. Someday."*

All three servants are gifted with something of immense value, awards delivered with two other unstated gifts: ***Trust*** **and** ***time.***

If the master wanted only to preserve his capital, he could have left his gold locked up and under guard. Instead, he distributes it to three agents of varying levels of ability and with no further instruction or expectations leaves town with an undetermined return date.

Let's put ourselves in the servants' position. We are also agents with our talents, and begin to realize with discovery and practice just how large these allocations are, and the level of effort required to bring them to fulfillment. These realizations can be empowering, inspiring, and motivating. We can leverage these feelings and our native energy to reach for the full flowering of what we have.

Alternatively, we can allow the knowledge of what we have and what it will take from us to arouse agoraphobic terrors scaring us back into the comfortable hole we cowered in before we realized what we had.

In Jesus' story, the actions of the three servants play out in ways uncannily mirroring real life.

- Servant One doubles his five-bag allocation to ten, a 100% Return On Investment.
- Servant Two doubles his two-bag allocation to four, also a 100% ROI.
- Servant Three buries the gold and loses nothing. Also gains nothing. 0% ROI.

When the master returns, the servants present themselves to account not only for their allocations but for the time and trust they were given.

Servant One receives lavish praise, a promise of greater responsibilities and allocations, and an invitation to share in the master's happiness.

Servant two, who delivered the same margin but only 40% of Servant One's actual profit, receives praise and promises *verbatim identical* to those of Servant One.

Servant Three, on the other hand, succumbed to fear and took measures to protect his master's wealth, making sure it was not exposed to any risk. In so doing, he guaranteed the outcome the master had *chosen against,* which was leaving his wealth idle under lock and key.

Worse, Three tries to *blame the master* for his choice. 'I knew that you are a hard man, harvesting where you have not sown and gathering where you have not scattered seed. So I was afraid and went out and hid your gold in the ground.'

The implication is the master is "hard" because he profits from the labor of others, going on vacation while his servants are left to do all the work. Perhaps Three had witnessed the praise and rewards lavished upon One and Two and, frustrated by what he perceived as the "unfairness" of the situation tried to justify himself in the face of what he saw coming.

To say Servant Three was "terminated with cause" is understatement. Being labeled "wick and lazy", stripped of his allocation and watching it handed to the servant who started and ended with the most was bad enough. But then he's thrown out into darkness. Jesus' Jewish audience would have heard this as the equivalent of being sent to Hell.

Whew. Harsh.

But not really. The results are no different than what would happen in a modern-day proprietary equities trading firm. Promotions and increases are, as they must be, performance-based. It's not only that the firm's purpose is to "make money". The firm would eventually cease to exist if they didn't operate this way. The "bottom feeders" in performance are fired and any capital they were working with is immediately transferred to the top dogs, who get more and more experience and eventually become full partners in the firm.

Many of Jesus' casual listeners may have nodded with comprehension and muttered "makes sense" as they recognized this real-world pattern. Of course that's how it would play out in a real business environment. I can see a humble listener speaking up, *"Teacher, what exactly are you saying to us?"*

I can see the Master replying in his cryptic fashion as he does at several points in the New Testament after telling his parables. *"Whoever has ears to hear, let them hear."* Considering how mixed his audience was in terms of their belief systems, spiritual maturity and familiarity with Jesus' previous parables, there could be no better reply.

This response might be annoying to some sign-seekers who just wanted a spoon-feeding of Jesus's words so they could pass judgment on his message. Eyes may have rolled and some even stomped off complaining about the "pointless story".

Others, not fully comprehending but hungry to learn, internalized the message. *I need to take this home and think about it. I need to remember it, repeat it, turn it over in my mind and put myself in the story.*

Those closest to Jesus, particularly those dozen or so who would shortly be joining him at the Last Supper, were expected to take away an interpretation unique to them. They had been , and in coming days would be, witnesses to unprecedented historical and spiritual events. They'd had authority conferred on them, and were expected not only to teach what the Master taught, but to do the miraculous things he did. Very familiar with their rabbi's teaching style, they would each be mulling over their individual "bags of gold" and how active they were in trading and gaining.

We know from scriptural context even his most intimate disciples did not yet fully understand what was coming, so they may not have discerned Jesus himself was the master who would soon "take a journey" and leave them entrusted with these gifts.

So we return to *our* place in the story.

We are also in varying statuses in our beliefs and levels of understanding. We too need to open our "ears to hear", and find the interpretation fitting us where we are.

Maybe you've never thought of your way with words or eye for detail or easy way with wood, numbers, stone, computers or canvas as a "bag of gold". You've certainly never thought of your modest gifts as being part of a zero-sum game where if you don't make the most of it, someone else will.

But that is precisely the case.

God, the Universe, or Whatever wants good things done and wants them done through the beings designed to do it. The Supreme Creator is "a hard man", harvesting where no sowing was done and gathering where nothing was scattered. If this wasn't true, why would Resistance even bother with us? We are agents here. The master is still away but is due to return soon. The date and time of his return is unknown to each of us because we can be taken out by a wayward Mack truck or an aggressive carcinoma, neither of which gives a rat's patootie about our preferred timeline.

Finding Your Place

The little corners we call "niches" are nothing more than categorized human needs, little pockets of demand seeking supply.

Your paradigm of creativity may be limited to a way to express yourself, to let off the steam of your creative impulses - an outlet. "I write for myself," or "I do this because it brings me joy."

This is important. It is good and right.

But it's only half of the equation of fully-flowered creativity.

What exactly does the doubling of the gold by the two "good and faithful" servants represent?

We call it impact. We call it value.

Those are reactions to what you've created, beyond your sense of accomplishment in just having created it.

Do you long to hear those words *"well done, good and faithful servant"* echoing in your mind? Today it's likely to be heard in the reviews and testimonials of those finding value in your work. Not for your ego's sake, but for *their* sake.

You've got to make it visible.

Today six billion people, or 73% of the world's population, connect to the internet every day. Most of them don't really have any money. Some of them have more than they know what to do with. They all have needs. They're all searching. Powerful algorithms are rapidly mastering the mathematics of connecting demand with supply.

All the niches will be filled, but by whom? *"For whoever has will be given more, and they will be given an abundance. Whoever does not have, even what they have will be taken from them."*

If even 0.00001% of those six billion people are in need of what you have, there are 600 people online right now who want to see it, read it, own it or consume it. If you don't connect with them and supply it, someone else will -

but they won't be able to do it in exactly the same way you could.

You may be thinking, *"what the heck would Jesus have known about the internet?"*

To which I'll reply "If he knew what was going to happen next Friday night, why not the twenty-first century?"

To quote him from another time and place,

> **"You are the light of the world. A town built on a hill cannot be hidden. Neither do people light a lamp and put it under a bowl. Instead they put it on its stand, and it gives light to everyone in the house. In the same way, let your light shine before others, that they may see your good deeds..."**   **Matt 5:14-16**

The point of this chapter is not to show Jesus is the best teacher, a prescient master of of universal truth and bottomless wisdom, although I believe those things are true and I'm more than a fan.

The point is, as you complete a five-day creative challenge and consider what to do next, an understanding of what you carry is crucial. If you've minimized your creative possessions by comparison or doubting their value, you may be overly exposed to catastrophic Resistance followed by a swift relapse and "re-tox" to your previous state. Worse, you may be vulnerable to putting yourself in Servant Three's cursed shoes even as you try to protect yourself from the loss and pain of criticism and temporary failure.

The impulse to *just bury it* can be overwhelming on some days, and easy to do. The distractions available to numb us into forgetfulness are bright, colorful, tasty and loud, appearing much more appealing than the dirt they really are.

Who aspires to have the words "wicked and lazy" applied to themselves? Others around you, even your Accountability Partners, may be too kind to say them - or at least, not in those words!

Ultimately, *5 Fearless Days* is a tool. Maybe a better term is weapon, or even a ballistic missile aimed at the hardened seals deposited over your potential through years of partial or full neglect.

By now, you know where you stand, and hopefully you see it as holy ground. It's a unique position, because no one can occupy the same space you can. This is true in literal and figurative ways.

You are in possession of certain concentrations of mental and spiritual gold that can't be mined or duplicated by anyone else. The original teller of the Parable of the Bags of Gold used precious metal coinage to represent these things because at the time it was the greatest concentration of value his hearers could comprehend.

You may take stock of your "allocation" and assume with humility, *"I must be a one-bagger."* Maybe that's all you can see at this point in your creative life. The message of the story is **whatever you're given can be much more, and how much you have at the end matters far more than what you began with.**

You are here to act and not be acted upon.

Your five-day challenge is the time to climb up to the arena and act. These are "fearless" days because you leave no time to entertain your anxieties and insecurities. It's time to double down on doubling up what you have.

The Eighth and final chapter of this book is about what happens next. These five days are not meant as an isolated experience or a tiny island in a sea of procrastination and stalled progress. If they're going to be more, certain steps must be taken.

ACTIONS TO COMPLETE BEFORE MOVING ON:

❑ Review one more time the text of The Parable of the Bags of Gold earlier in this chapter. Write below the gifts and allocations you feel are your own "bags of gold":

____

____

____

____

____

❑ Ponder for a moment or few minutes about each of the questions below:

Do you feel a responsibility or internal pressure to develop what you have?

Have you felt sympathy for the fate of Servant Three or fear he might be the character representing YOU in the story?

Ponder how an understanding of this story can provide strength against the specific forms of Resistance you face.

Never Break The Chain

If you're looking back from here on your first *5 Fearless Days* challenge, I sincerely hope you've surprised yourself.

You were asked to set an objective about 20% beyond your perceived ability for the time frame. If you've done as much, you've learned something important about yourself: You can stretch without breaking. That's called growth. It can't be taken away from you now, and unless you forget about it or label it a fluke, it's only the beginning.

This is cause for celebration. Start with your AP. Take them to lunch, dinner, or whatever seems appropriate. Next, make sure your family and friends are in on your success, and pop the proverbial (or literal) cork in front of them. Then, trumpet it out across social media, stating exactly what you've done and the time it took. You'll be surprised at how many people will engage with these celebratory posts because they are all too rare.

Don't be tempted to keep it quiet because, well, you're "not really done with anything yet." Not true. You are a *finisher* on an unprecedented scale. You've proven something previously unproven. Bring visibility to what you've done. It will fortify your momentum and get people asking about when they can see your work published or available.

Remember, beyond expression it's about impact.

You've just completed an adventure with many of the ancient elements of an epic. You set out to do something beyond your abilities. Then you did it against the rocks and monsters sliding down the steep slope of your high-Y axis toward you. You took them on as they came. You weren't alone. You drew on the support of your AP and the principles in this book, including a written contract anchoring you to your purpose.

Your adventure is now in the archives, but you're just getting started. Indiana Jones did some amazing things in his quest for the *Lost Ark*, but he went on to the *Temple of Doom*, the *Last Crusade* and (come on, they weren't *that* bad) the *Kingdom of the Crystal Skull* and *The Dial of Destiny*.

The best adventures come in sequence. They have sequels. Are you a one-hit wonder or a franchise player? Only sequential performance can lead to exponential progress.

A part of this *segue* into the next phase of your adventures are the new fears bound to materialize. Upgraded and sophisticated forms of Resistance you've never faced before but have the same potential to send you scrambling back to the hidey-hole of a plush comfort zone.

Let's review and rephrase the two risks introduced at the end of Chapter Six, the fears most likely lined up to obliterate the gains of your five hard-fought days:

1. I'm going back to real life now. Job. Family. Home
    life. The same distractions. The challenge was
    exciting and I surprised myself, but what's stopping
    me from having the same life a week from now that I
    had a week ago?

2. I'm not really finished with anything. I have a rough
    draft, and I kept the terms of my contract. But it's
    crap. It needs so much work before I can ship it. So I
    probably won't.

These aren't fake monsters. They're not figments of your imagination. They wield all the intelligence of your own cerebral cortex, and should be visualized as tangible forces working hard to stop you cold. They will infect you, and without treatment they will spread.

What you've started matters. Why would anything try to stop you if it didn't? Stop pointing the finger at yourself as the problem. The only thing you've done wrong is to accept bad ideas. The first step in rejecting them is to recognize them for what they are: Parasites. Foreign bodies your creative immune system should expel with extreme prejudice.

Let's call them Virulent Bad ideas (VBI's). You believe them because "everyone else" does. Or because you accepted them early and life seems to have proven them out. They've become self-fulfilling prophecies. They're the clear water and you're the goldfish.

We'll take on these two because they're common to many coming off their first intense challenge, people staring at what by the numbers is an amazing pile of output, but output that won't win any prizes in its current state.

These two VBI's are closely related. Let's examine each.

VBI #1: My life before is my life after and I don't *have time.*

This one is as true as you allow it to be. You know you've made a leap.

When Neil Armstrong's boots hit the lunar surface in 1969, he was smart enough to recognize his feet had just traveled a few inches from the lowest rung of a metal stepladder. The "giant leap" part of his statement referred to the 240,000 miles, 400,000 smart people and the vast, previously unvalidated pile of math and science enabling him to be there, on the moon's surface, alive and breathing oxygen.

You look at what you've just accomplished and think, "sure, I jumped. But gravity brought me right back down to where I was before."

Not true if your jump was uphill.

You've landed on higher ground.

Your job now is not only to maintain your position, but to climb higher, maybe in smaller steps, toward a summit still out of sight, blocked by obstacles ahead.

The difference now is you're a certified climber. Before, you might list your roles like father, wife, sister, son, manager, plumber, student, and follow it with "writer" or "artist" in a smaller font at the bottom. You know, the thing you do in your "spare time" when all other demands are met and everyone with a claim on your time is happy with you.

Now you're smarter. You're enlightened. You realize YOU are the primary claimant on your time and energy. For a few days, you had a Contract with yourself and you fulfilled it. This didn't nullify your other active contracts, written and unwritten, made previously with your domestic partner, your offspring, employer, or the bank holding the lien on your car.

You've discovered your creative identity is a part of your life deserving the same font size as all other roles. It's not a hobby or side-hustle. Sure, you maximized it for a few days, moved it to the front while other roles took a back seat. It needed your attention, your assertion, your recognition. It needed time and space and you delivered.

So now what?

Remember who you are, and how you've changed. A creator still creating. A climber still climbing. A finisher with many more finishes ahead.

Combine this attitude with an unbroken string of daily activity leading up to your next five-day challenge, even if it's a year away.

I'm very serious about two vital keys here:

1. You must do some kind of work on a creative project ***every day***.

2. Your next five-day challenge should always be on your calendar.

These are the fruits of long experience. Can you set aside your role as a husband or mother for even one day? No. Even if you're on a business trip around the world in Indonesia, you make contact with your loved ones before you sleep.

I'm talking about a five-minute floor. Bare minimum. Write or code a paragraph. Sketch a face. Outline a simple landing page. Write about the next steps in your journal. **Never underestimate the power of uninterrupted consecutivity, however small.**

Skipping one day, one circadian spin, one night of the sun going down and the covers being pulled up on a day without acknowledging the "bags of gold" in your possession puts you at risk. *Two days* skipped is the psychological equivalent of bombing your progress back to the stone age.

Come on, Mike. You've been quite the drama queen in this book, but this takes the cake. Two missed days are that bad?

Two missed days are that bad.

This is the single-most important lesson of my life so far —a life, by the way, which I spent the larger part of not following the creative thread now running through each of my days. Lose the thread and it won't be long before you drop the needle. Imagine yourself standing atop a ten-foot haystack looking for a needle as the sun dips below the horizon.

Some days, you'll only get five minutes. But you can't be honest and say "I didn't even have five minutes" at the same time. Other days, you'll have five hours. The length of time matters far less than the consistency and the consecutivity.

Whose fault is it if you miss your five minutes and therefore the day? Think hard about this. We're talking about *five minutes*. Can you get up five minutes earlier or stay up five minutes later?

Silly question.

VBI #2: What I made during my challenge isn't very good, so it was a waste.

Cal Newport's wonderful book *Deep Work* deserves a spot on the shelf next to Steven Pressfield's pithy works. Newport introduces a powerful formula:

High-Quality Work Produced = (Time Spent) x (Intensity of Focus)

You spent the time, and you made your focus intense.

Now you're looking at what you've created, and you're questioning the formula. Where's the "high-quality work"?

Instead, what you've got is a bolus of messy draft or unfinished WIP you'd be embarrassed to show your mother. Sure, there are some nuggets. There are some flashes of brilliance in there, things you can use and build on. But overall, you're looking at a lot more work to mold it into something you can bring to market.

Yes! You're right, and that's right where you want to be.

Anything done is vastly superior to anything not done.

Remember in Chapter Six where I talked about the five-day challenge I did resulting in 37,901 words of fiction draft? Would it surprise you to learn no one but me has ever read those words, the draft was never finished, and a week later I pivoted into a completely different non-fiction project?

The purpose and parameters of this particular challenge were unique. I started on Page 1 with an idea and vague outline of what was to be the first volume of a trilogy. I didn't even know how the story would end. The idea was to take what I had and just roll with it, writing an exploratory draft to see where it would take me.

In the rear-view mirror, this was ill-advised for me as a writer. Beginning *without* the end in mind is a Virulent Bad Idea in itself, and it became more true the more I wrote. Destiny and foreshadowing are powerful elements of a heroic story, and you can see how lack of clarity around ultimate outcomes would start causing problems.

So, do I regret the hours and days invested in that challenge? Do I resent losing them from my PTO bank, or missing out on the sunburn I never got at the beach? Not at all. Here are just a few things I picked up in the "plus column":

- I proved to myself I could generate draft at a rate of over 7,000 words-per-day average, which surprised and inspired me.

- I found the right personal cadence for my "pomodoro" timing and the importance of physical activity during the breaks.

- I discovered the power of momentum and flow in deep work and how plot and how characters can take on lives of their own in this immersion, even when you're not writing.

- As I reviewed my draft, I found many gems of description, dialogue and world-building bolstering my confidence working in the genre.

- Ultimately I came away with the knowledge the next step was not to continue this draft, but to take a break and come back to the project with fresh eyes and a willingness to build the foundational, end-to-end structure upon which the next, better draft will hang.

Wasted time? Hardly. If I hadn't done the challenge I would have ZERO of the items listed above. My subconscious would still be haunted by anxiety and uncertainty around the whole idea of writing such a story. I'd still be stuck. Instead, I came away knowing exactly what my next steps should be and I'm set up for more and better future challenges.

Such challenge outcomes should never be treated as "dead ends". Catalog your gains as I did above. This is what habitual daily journaling is for. You can't focus on anything for 120 hours and not come away with a long list of benefits.

Accept the fruit of your challenges won't always be taken immediately to market, and some of it will never see the light of day. Regardless, these fruits are essential iterations of your creative self. These "failed" efforts act as points on a map leading you to increasingly optimal results with practice.

On the other hand, you may be quite happy with the output of your challenge. You know it's not finished or polished, but you have a clear view of what needs to be done to make it launch-ready. As you do your first review, a mental list of what needs to be done may start building toward a staggering wave of overwhelm. You pair this with the random chunks of "confetti time" you see on your calendar and it seems like too much being shoehorned into too little.

Stop.

This is where you take a break. You're out of challenge mode now. Go get some ice cream. Or, to avoid a violation of your dietary commitment, maybe a small bowl of chilled hummus with a handful of baby carrots.

Take a walk. Watch a movie. Have a long talk with a friend or partner about something entirely unrelated.

Don't lose the thread. Stick with the advice above addressing VBI #1 and spend at least five minutes each day doing something creative, but focused on something other than this particular project. Give it time as we'll explore below.

Again, you're right where you want to be. It may feel overwhelming at the moment, but it's also exciting, isn't it? You know what you need to do next. Well, you will once you "wrap your head around it", which is the next step after this brief reset and break.

Maintaining Momentum - The Source of "More Time"

What you created during your *5 Fearless Days* needs a rest. Your identity as a consistent and reliable creator does not.

When applied to the work you've done, there are two distinct definitions of "finished" to keep distinct:

- At the end of a successful challenge, you're "finished" if your goal was 10,000 words and you now have 10,000 or more words. This is a mighty accomplishment.

- You're not anywhere near "finished" with the larger project, which might be 50,000 words, edited, polished and ready for publication.

A creative life is a life of milestones, some of which are headlong sprints with "rough" work, and others highly focused completion goals culminating in bringing work to market. Every project has multiple phases and cycles. It's easy to get addicted to starting new things, harder to get hooked on finishing them. The closer you get to a finish for every start, the stronger you become as a creator.

Fearless Hack: Get addicted to a 1:1 start/finish ratio and you've created a superpower compressing time which has built many enduring legacies and fortunes.

Unless you're financially independent and light on family responsibilities, you're not free to execute a five-day challenge every week or even every month. You have to be strategic about it, maintain a long perspective and be content with scraps when there's no feast on the table. You may only get 2-3 five-day challenge opportunities in a good year.

That's okay.

For most busy people who have discovered the power of five-day commitments, the distribution of creative work time falls into three buckets:

1. A third gets done during dedicated and focused multi-day intensives like *5 Fearless Days* challenges.
2. A third gets done on Saturday and Sunday mornings between 4am and 10am as the rest of the world "sleeps in". That's up to 12 hours per week!
3. The remaining third gets done during "confetti time", the odds and ends of a life with multiple roles and responsibilities ranging from 5 minutes to several hours.

Omitting any of the three buckets could result in your projects taking 50% longer to complete.

The mistake too many inexperienced creatives make is to assume #3 is the only bucket they have. It tends to look like the deepest bucket and many have built fortunes and legacies from this bucket alone. Bucket #2 is frequently neglected because we all want to sleep in like everyone else. It's been a hard week! Bucket #1 is often ignored simply because people don't know it's a thing unless they get their hands on this book.

Am I really suggesting you get up and start working at 4:00 AM on weekends? It"s my schedule seven days a week. Without it, this book would have taken at least two months longer to produce. It requires a bed time no later than 9:00 PM, also seven days a week. Crazy? If you say so. But I still get 7 hours of sleep each night and two uninterrupted mini-challenges of five hours every week. A nice bucket #2.

Your schedule is yours and I'm not going to tell you when to sleep, wake, eat, and create. The point is, your complaint of "I don't have time!" is going to draw some serious side-eye from me and others who know better. You decide which parts of your routine belong on the sacrificial altar – is it the drinks and socializing on Friday night making Saturday mornings a sunk cost? The 3.5-hour Sunday football game exposing you to 1.5 hours of advertising?

The clock and calendar are yours; do with them what you will. You're an agent.

Building the Bridge

We've reviewed your main sources of time, which along with effort, talent and trust in your own word are the elements of growth and finished work. It's time to return to the challenge just completed.

You've got an important body of work in rough form. Here are some proven steps for how to proceed from Day Six onward:

1. Let it rest for 10-14 days. Don't even look at it. Instead, enjoy your promised rewards and move on to something either beyond the scope of the work or completely unrelated. For example, if you successfully drafted Chapters 1-5 of a book, you could do research or drafting for Chapter 6 during this time. Never less than 5 minutes per day as a rock-bottom minimum, and you shouldn't go more than a few days without some 25-minute or longer blocks.

2. During this "rest" period, examine the next 90 days and plot out your major and minor time blocks. This does NOT count as creative work. It may be

weeks or months before you can pull off another five-day fully immersive challenge. Until then you're working with what you've got, which could be as little as five minutes or as much as 5-10 hours on a weekend day or holiday.

3.   Schedule your next 5-day challenge ASAP. I hope you've seen the value in making space for at least one of these annually. Yes, sometimes you need a vacation. You also need to challenge yourself for at least five days.

4.   Come back to the work done during your challenge after 10-14 days when you can set aside 90 minutes or more for it. Review it from a "10,000 foot" perspective, skimming each section or chapter and taking notes either in a separate notebook or on a split screen. This process allows you to "capture" new ideas and improvements. Once they're documented, they don't need to take up mental space and trigger overwhelm and anxiety. DO NOT listen to voices encouraging you to feel overwhelmed by what remains to be done or underwhelmed by the initial quality of what you see in front of you.

5.   Set specific goals for how much revision you'll get done each week. Be slightly more realistic than you would be for an immersive challenge period. **Shorter chunks of time under 30 minutes are more about consistency than productivity.** It may feel like you're not getting much done during each piece of this "confetti time", but they add up.

6. Target a completion date for your next draft or publication/market readiness. It's okay to give yourself deadlines - heaven knows everyone else is willing to hand them to you. It's an important part of the promise-keeping equation and building the kind of honesty that brings results. Just remember those ultimate deadlines are meant to be flexible and your DAILY show-up and completion objectives are far more important.

7. AI can be a useful partner in creating your between-challenge schedule. Open a chat and tell the model all about your life, roles, responsibilities, creative work and objectives. Ask it to take into account the latest research on creative psychology and deep work and list out your preferences for Pomodoro intervals and breaks. Then let it create a suggested 90-day schedule.

Make your creative work an integral part of your everyday life. It's a little like being a gold miner: You'll spend most of your time on your claim gathering flecks and little nuggets from among mountains of rock. On rare occasions you'll stumble into rich veins of preciousness seeming to go on and on. Eureka!

Your life beats the mining analogy because the value comes from both the planned time and the unexpected illumination from ideas. You see your next challenge coming up in June, but on April 14th while deep into a 45-minute block between dinner and bedtime when everyone else is ogling Netflix, something special emerges from the soup of your mind. You capture it and incorporate it into the day's or an upcoming day's work. These moments fuel you through to the next session.

Then, as the time approaches for your next *5 Fearless Days*, you'll look forward to it with a stomach-fluttering anticipation. Who needs Disney World when you've got five days to yourself and you're rolling into it with a full head of steam?

One more time: You're here on this earth to act and not be acted upon. So let your light so shine. Take your bags of gold, multiply them and bring them back to approval and praise. You're here to serve. To stand and deliver.

Fearlessly.

This book was born out of a true passion for human creativity. Why do I care so much? As I stated in my Preface, I'm convinced we as a human race have created nearly all of the problems plaguing us here in the 21st century. We also hold the keys to creating the solutions to said problems.

It won't just be math and science and government and AI bailing us out of the messes we've gotten ourselves into. The solutions will come from posts and books and podcasts not yet published. Art yet to arrive in physical form or have impact because it's still just a dream. Content living only in embryonic form because its parent minds haven't made time or space for it to come into the world.

There's so much to do, so much to see and so much to learn in our world. For the first time in history, the buffet of consumables stretches out of sight into infinity, and we can choose to sample a bite from a thousand tasty side-dishes or tuck into the heartiest entrees. Technology is designed to save us time and give us access to more, resulting in overwhelm, over-stimulation and the perception of having less time than our ancestors, which is ridiculous.

Once we get past the first question of "why create anything, when everything has already been done?" we realize we have more raw material than any previous generation to forge solutions to the increasingly complex problems we face.

I've chosen to spend more of my limited time creating than consuming. The more people who do this, the better the world will be.

You can unplug from the problem and become a part of the solution.

It starts with a decision and a commitment.

Then 5 Fearless Days.

Appendix

RESOURCES SUPPORTING YOUR MOMENTUM

This book was drafted using the principles contained in this book.

How's that for a "chicken and egg" paradox?

Writing *Five Fearless Days* was not my first rodeo, nor will it be my last. The ideas this book contains have been proven out over time and experience, and will continue to be refined over time and subsequent challenges - both my own and those completed by people like you. Future editions of this book will reflect those refinements. But there are certain resources a book can't provide.

I've seen reviews on self-help books expressing things like "the whole book is just a big infomercial for what the author is selling." I get it. No one wants to buy anything just to find out it's a loss leader for the real thing.

If you've read this far, you know this book is more than a lead magnet. It was written with the sole purpose of providing *everything you need* to feel empowered to complete your own five-day challenges and make creative breakthroughs independently, with no further investment beyond your time and effort.

Having said that, some of those reading this book are looking for more advanced support and any additional resources available to ensure their momentum.

5fearlessdays.com

The website is a hub supporting everything in this book, and will be in continual development. There you'll find free resources like a computer-based (no phones allowed in challenges!) planner that generates and gamifies five-day challenges for you based on your preferences, and a similar app to plan and guide 90-day bridges between challenges. You'll get access to my free newsletter, *Create or Die*, which provides ongoing support for the creative process.

This book is focused on helping you prepare and execute five-day creative challenges on your own. What's missing is *community*. At 5fearlessdays.com, you'll find a portal to a growing tribe of like-minded people looking to swap AP duties for each other and share the joys and sorrows of their challenges. I'm organizing and leading *5 Fearless Days* cohorts of 10-20 people completing their challenges on the same days, with brief, supportive video calls to kick off each of your five days.

If this sounds like the place for you, or you're just curious to see what's happening on the inside, please stop by!

Great Books Supporting *5 Fearless Days* Challenges

Steven Pressfield, *The War of Art*, 2002

Steven Pressfield, *Turning Pro*, 2012

Cal Newport, *Deep Work*, 2016

Stephen R. Covey, *The 7 Habits of Highly Effective People*, 1989

30-Day Training Program to Prepare for Your First 5 Fearless Days Challenge

This program can also be found as a downloadable PDF complete with checklists and worksheets at 5fearlessdays.com.

This program works better than the 10-day program outlined in Chapter Five for nearly everyone, but in particular for busy professionals starting from high digital stimulation, little existing focused creative work practice, or who want a sustainable, gradual preparation. Think of your mind as a computer with far too many browser tabs open. This program will help you with your "browser hygiene" and the process of removing countless distractions and irrelevant inputs.

IMPORTANT: What you do during your training work blocks is far less important than the fact that you are following instructions. As you progress through the training, you may choose to do something to prepare yourself for (research or practice), which dovetails with or advances on what you have set as your contractual challenge commitment.

Timeline: 30 consecutive days leading up to your scheduled five-day challenge.

Commitment: 30 to 90 minutes per day of deliberate practice.

Key Weekly Themes

Week	Days	Focus
Week 1	1-7	Awareness, gentle digital detox, sleep
Week 2	8-14	Building core persistence stamina
Week 3	15-21	Digital detox, boredom tolerance and emotional regulation.
Week 4	22-30	Sprint simulation, identity work and taper into challenge.

Week 1: Awareness, Gentle Digital Detox, and Sleep (Days 1-7)

Daily Anchors (every day this week)

1. **Morning page** (write for 5-10 minutes)
   a. What matters most today?
   b. When will I have the opportunity for my focus block?
   c. What's one way I'll practice being less stimulated?
2. **One short focus block of 25 minutes**
   a. Single task, no switching, personal device out of sight and sound
3. **Evening wind-down** (30 minutes before bed)
   a. NO SCREENS within 30 minutes of bed
   b. Substitute reading physical book, journaling, stretching, or conversation

Days 1-2: Device and Attention Audit

- Track all device checks for 48 hours using hash marks on a sticky note
- Count checks at the end of each day
- Identify triggers: Boredom, anxiety, habit, fatigue, awkward social situations

Days 3-4: Light Notification Pruning

- Turn off notifications for social media, news and entertainment apps
- Keep only calls and essential work notifications

Days 5-7: Offline Micro-Retreats

- 10-20 minutes each day in low-stimulation activity
- Options: Walk without phone, sit quietly, stretching, read paper book

Week 1 Reflections (use as morning page prompts)

How fragmented is my attention right now, on a scale of 1-10?

What surprised me about my device check count?

What did I notice with 30 minutes of no screens before bed?

What's one digital habit I'm ready to permanently change this week?

Week 1 Checklist

Day	Morning Page	Focus Block	Evening Wind-Down	Theme Task
Day 1	☐	☐	☐	☐
Day 2	☐	☐	☐	☐
Day 3	☐	☐	☐	☐
Day 4	☐	☐	☐	☐
Day 5	☐	☐	☐	☐
Day 6	☐	☐	☐	☐
Day 7	☐	☐	☐	☐

Week 2: Building Core Persistence and Stamina (Days 8-14)

This Week's Targets

- 4 days with at least 2 x 25-minute focus blocks
- 1 day with a 45-minute focus block

Daily Elements

Focus Block Progression

- Gradually move from 1 block to 2 blocks for at least 4 days this week
- Always on meaningful tasks (not busywork)

- Use a timer and honor your commitment

Digital Detox Step

- 1 evening with your phone in another room after 7pm
- Another day with a 4-hour chunk of waking hours with no devices

Week 2 Reflections (use as journal prompts)

How did my focus and persistence stamina change from Day 8 to Day 14?

What time of day do I focus best?

What happened during my 4-hour device-free window? (feelings, insights, challenges)

What's getting easier?

Week 2 Checklist

Day	Focus Blocks	Detox Step	45-Minute Bock (1 Required
Day 8	☐	☐	☐
Day 9	☐	☐	☐
Day 10	☐	☐	☐
Day 11	☐	☐	☐
Day 12	☐	☐	☐
Day 13	☐	☐	☐
Day 14	☐	☐	☐

Total focus minutes this week:_________

Best focus block (day and time):_________

Week 3: Advanced Digital Detox, Boredom Tolerance and Emotional Skills (Days 15-21)

Weekly Targets

- 3 days with 2 x 45-minute focus blocks
- 1 day with a 90-minute continuous focus block
- At least 3 "analog evenings" with no devices after dinner

Daily Mindset Practice

Days 15-16: Boredom is Training

Use small pockets of boredom (waiting in line, elevator rides, breaks, walking from your car to shops or appointments) to simply observe without reaching for your phone. Notice the discomfort. Stay with it.

Days 17-18: Feel an Urge Without Obeying It

Practice urge-surfing when you want to check devices, succumb to half an hour of entertainment or eat something pleasant but unhealthy. Imagine the urge as a wave. It rises, peaks, and falls. You don't have to act on it.

Days 19-21: Build a Challenge-Ready Nervous System

Notice your body and mind adapting to longer focus periods and less stimulation. Observe the discomfort, itchiness, and nerves, but also the growing expansion of time and your ability to get more creative work done in less of it.

Start Ritual

- Same time of day, same space: 3 deep breaths, set timer, define a single clear outcome, could be as simple as a single page of your journal.

- Protect your work blocks from all communication, using an autoresponder and calendar blocks as necessary.

Digital Detox: "Analog Evenings" (at least three times this week):

- No devices after dinner
- Alternatives: reading physical non-fiction books, journaling, planning, conversation, creative hobbies
- If possible, move your phone and charging station to another room and leverage "Do Not Disturb" mode for your sleep time.

Emotional Skills Practice

When anxiety or FOMO surrounding being offline appears:

1. Journal - "What am I afraid will happen?"
2. Journal - "What happened the last time I was offline for hours?"
3. Use brief breath work: 4 counts in, hold 4, exhale 6, hold 2 (repeat 5x)

Week 3 Journal Reflections

How has my relationship with boredom changed this week?

What did I learn when I practiced "feeling the urge without obeying it"?

What happened during my "Analog Evenings"?

What fears about device separation are getting smaller?

Day	Mindset Theme	Focus Blocks	Start Ritual	Analog Evening (at least 3)
Day 15	☐	☐	☐	☐
Day 16	☐	☐	☐	☐
Day 17	☐	☐	☐	☐
Day 18	☐	☐	☐	☐
Day 19	☐	☐	☐	☐
Day 20	☐	☐	☐	☐
Day 21	☐	☐	☐	☐

Week 4: Challenge Simulation, Identity Work and Taper (Days 22-30)

Challenge Simulation (Day 22, 23, 24, 25, or 26 as Scheduled)

- Select one of days 22-26 for a 4-6 hour time frame to simulate full *5 Fearless Days* Challenge rules:

- 4-6 Focus Blocks of 45-minutes each followed by 15-minute breaks

- Challenge rules in effect: Minimal or no notifications, phone out of room, scheduled check-in windows only.

- Before bed the evening of the simulation, answer these questions in your journal:

- What worked so well I want to copy it during my five-day challenge?
- What broke or caused friction?
- What scares me or made me uncomfortable?
- How can I resolve these issues before my challenge starts next week?

Protocol For Other days 22-28

For the other days leading up to days 29-30, target the following minimums as you prepare for your 5 Fearless Days of total commitment:

- Start ritual at the same time and place every day if possible
- At least two 45-minute focus blocks daily

Incorporate the work in the next section into this week's focus blocks.

Identity and Environment Preparations

Write a one-page answer to: **"Who I Become During My *5 Fearless Days* Challenge"**

Describe in detail a full ideal day of your challenge:

- Waking up
- First work block
- A moment of struggle and how you respond
- Lunch and rest breaks
- Afternoon blocks
- Evening wind-down
- Going to bed feeling proud and accomplished

Read this visualization aloud at some point every day from now through Day 30.

Environment: By day 28, complete the setup of your challenge workspace:

- Remove all unnecessary items from desk
- Prepare analog captures tools (notebooks, index cards, pens)
- Set up printed schedules and checklists
- If using a computer, set up the online *5 Fearless Days* Planner
- Finalize device plan: Where? Who? How will emergencies be handled?

Cognitive Taper: Days 29-30

Limit your focus blocks to one medium flow block of no more than 45-60 minutes on both of these days. Outside of these, focus on lighter preparatory tasks:

- Process and fold laundry
- Line up clothing choices for all five days of your challenge to avoid decision fatigue
- Grocery shopping and any advanced meal preparation required
- Arrangements for child care and backup as well as emergency contacts
- Touching base with and setting expectations for Accountability Partner(s)

Maintain "social media and entertainment silence" for at least a 6-hour stretch on both of these days.

Day 30: Final Contract Review

Review the contract you wrote up and signed when you first committed to a 5 Fearless Days challenge. Your progress during your training program may require you to move the goal posts for your challenge. You may have learned some things about yourself inspiring you to aspire to more (or less) for these five days.

For example, if your original contractual obligation was to write 100 pages of the first draft of a book, you may already have completed 40 pages of draft during your 22 hours of work focus blocks during this training program. It may now be clear to you that you can complete 120 pages of draft during your five-day challenge, making your total for 35 days 160 pages.

There is nothing wrong with tearing up one contract and replacing it with another, as long as:

- You immediately replace it with another, improved contract

- You sign and date it again

- You have the buy-in of your AP (if your AP is not available for a physical signature, simply text them a photo of the contract and capture their reply)

Week 4 Checklist

Key Task	Complete
4-6 Hour Challenge Simulation	☐
Simulation Journal Reflection	☐
Write "Who I become..." and read aloud at least 4 days	☐
Challenge environment workspace setup	☐
Preparatory tasks (groceries, laundry, contacts) complete	☐
Cognitive taper (limit to a single focus block on days 29-30	☐
6 hours of entertainment silence days 29-30	☐
Final Contract review and re-signing (if applicable)	☐
Touch base and set expectations with AP(s)	☐

Wrapping It Up

Completing this program will prepare you in most ways for a successful five-day challenge. Most ways. If it's your first time, you will likely face things only the full experience will bring on. On the eve of your challenge, feelings of nervous anticipation are normal. Thoughts like "what am I getting myself into?" or "am I really doing this?" will pop up. Just "smile and wave" as they arise and pass like drifting balloons.

You chose this.

You decided.

You committed.

You are a person of integrity and you will finish.

As you go to sleep on the night of Day 30, drift off with confidence that if you've changed during these past 30 days, you ain't seen nothin' yet. These next 5 will amaze you.

Troubleshooting Your Training and/or Challenge

"Most obstacles melt away when we make up our minds to walk boldly through them." — Orison Swett Marden

You can expect problems, resistance, and opposition whenever you set out to take bold action. This 30-day training program, and the commitment to engage in a 5 Fearless Days challenge, certainly qualify as bold action. Here are some of the most common, and bold responses for each.

If You Miss a Day

The Truth: It happens. It really doesn't matter whose fault it is, even if you know it's yours and yours alone. One missed day doesn't erase the capacity you've built up because progress is not linear. The key is to recommit and persist.

Action Steps:

- Don't try to "make up" the missed day by adding together both days' workload

- Simple resume where you left off, skipping the missed day
- If you've missed 2+ days in a row without extreme mitigating circumstances, your commitment is in question. Set aside your next work block to spend thinking and journaling about the hard question: ***How much does my creative life and work mean to me?***

If a Work Focus Block Feels Impossible

The Truth: You need to be ready to feel discomfort. Impossible is not the same as uncomfortable. Ask yourself, "Am I tired, hungry, or overstimulated?" While this training is designed to reduce the odds of those feelings, you may need to take one or more of the following steps.

Action Steps:
- Shorten the block (15 minutes instead of 25, etc.)
- Check the basics: Hydration, food, sleep
- Try a different time of day or workspace
- Lower the challenge level of the task temporarily

If Device Anxiety Spikes

The Truth: This is normal. Allow your nervous system to adjust to lower stimulation by enduring it. This, too, shall pass.

Action Steps:
- Use the breathing protocol: 4 counts in, hold 4, exhale 6, hold 2 (repeated 5x)

- Journal while in block: "What am I afraid will happen if I'm offline?"
- Set a scheduled device check-in window (e.g. "I'll check messages at 5pm)
- Remind yourself: "I've been offline for (x) hours before. Nothing broke."

If Thoughts of the Upcoming Challenge are Feeling Overwhelming

The Truth: You're not preparing for 5 Perfect Days. You're preparing to ignore all fears and leap forward, which is proven doable by countless creative people before you. You're preparing to be capable. Trust the process.

Action Steps:

- Review a previous journal entry or write a new one describing the "why" behind your decision to do this challenge
- Focus on visualizing just the first hour of Day One, instead of the full five days
- Have a live or phone conversation with your AP about your concerns
- Click into 5fearlessdays.com, navigate to the Community. You'll find people there who know exactly what you're going through.
- Remember: This is not a prison sentence. You can revise or adjust at any time during your challenge. That's not quitting.

Did you find this book helpful? Your review on Amazon will make it visible to other creators. This QR code will take you directly to the review page.

Download your free gifts at:

www.5fearlessdays.com